D1552145

A Teacher's Guide to

STICK UP FOR YOURSELF!

A 10-Part Course in Self-Esteem and Assertiveness for Kids

by
Gerri Johnson, M.S.Ed.
Gershen Kaufman, Ph.D.
Lev Raphael, Ph.D.

Free Spirit
PUBLISHING

ISBN 0–915793–31–8

10 9 8 7 6 5 4 3

Printed in the United States of America

Cover design by MacLean & Tuminelly
Book design by Mark My Word

Free Spirit Publishing Inc.
400 First Avenue North, Suite 616
Minneapolis, MN 55401
(612) 338–2068

CONTENTS

INTRODUCTION

About This Course . . . .

This is the Teacher's Guide to *Stick Up For Yourself! Every Kid's Guide to Personal Power and Positive Self-Esteem* by Gershen Kaufman, Ph.D. and Lev Raphael, Ph.D. It provides a complete course for helping upper-elementary and middle school-age young people build self-esteem, become more self-aware, and develop and practice assertiveness skills. It is designed to be implemented as a comprehensive self-esteem curriculum for the classroom setting. It can be used in other group settings as well.

Complete instructions for the ten sessions are included. Each session draws upon material in *Stick Up For Yourself*, and students are asked to read portions of the book before and/or during each session.

The Teacher's Guide also includes suggestions for additional curriculum-related activities and a list of resources for teachers or group leaders.

Before you begin teaching this course, we recommend that you read these introductory pages, as well as the section titled "Getting Ready" on pages 5 – 8.

How the Sessions Are Organized . . . .

There are ten sessions in this course. A list of session topics is found on page 98 in the Appendix, along with the reading assignment for each session. You may want to make copies of this page to hand out to group members at the first session and to send to parents. (The list of sessions, as well as other forms found in the Appendix in this Teacher's Guide, may be reproduced.)

Time Requirements

The sessions were developed to use in time blocks of approximately thirty to forty-five minutes. The actual time required will vary somewhat depending on the amount of discussion. As you teach the course, you may want to keep track of the amount of time each session takes so that you have this information when you teach the course with another group.

General Guidelines

1. It is important to become familiar with the entire course before you conduct the first session.

   It is a good idea to practice using the tools yourself so that you are able to model them for the students. For example, if you start writing your own Happiness List (see pages 24 – 26) and I-Did-It List each day (see pages 56 – 57), you'll find you have examples to use in the sessions in which those tools are discussed.

2. Before beginning each session, be certain you have the materials available. The materials are listed separately at the beginning of each session in the Teacher's Guide.

3. As you plan for a session, think about things you can do to adapt the activities to the specific needs of your class and relate the examples to their interests.

   Sometimes you will want to change an activity or example in order to relate the course more directly to the needs of your particular class. You may decide to ask additional questions or to substitute questions. You may also want to draw examples from your personal experiences to give the course vitality.

   The wide margins in this Teacher's Guide allow you to write down additional questions to ask, personal experiences to help stimulate discussion, or notes on how you might want to change an activity.

4. Be sure to let parents know what you are doing in the course and invite their questions before, during, and after the course. (See "Informing and Involving Parents," page 5.)

Desired Learner Outcomes

What do you want the students to be able to do as a result of this session? That is the question the Learner Outcomes are meant to answer. Desired Learner Outcomes for each session are given at the beginning of the instructions for each session. Each activity in the session was developed to provide an opportunity to meet one or more of the outcomes.

During some sessions, you may choose to add or substitute an activity. For example, one activity may not relate to your class's needs at that particular time, and you may want to change it. As long as you keep in mind the desired outcomes, it is possible to substitute activities. Let the Learner Outcomes guide your planning.

Evaluation Suggestions . . . .

There are two types of student evaluation to consider: a *self-evaluation* by each student, and an overall *course evaluation*.

In the first session, students are asked to identify and describe in their notebooks particular situations in which they would like to learn to stick up for themselves. Their self-evaluation at the end of the course could involve asking them to read what they wrote during the first session and then decide, for themselves, whether they reached their goals. It might be helpful in the last session to have them list new ways they are learning to stick up for themselves. This will help them integrate their experience and realize what they have accomplished.

Whatever other means of evaluation you use, we recommend that the students evaluate their own progress and that this evaluation be for their information, not yours.

A course evaluation, on the other hand, will help you obtain feedback on the effectiveness of the course as a whole. A sample evaluation form is found on page 109 in the Appendix. The evaluation can be useful for planning future courses and for helping you decide how you might follow up after the course.

Your Role as Teacher . . . .

In this course, the teaching role may be somewhat different than what you are accustomed to. You will structure the activities and organize the physical setting as you do in other teaching situations. But the students, in a sense, determine the content. It is their life experiences that will form the basis for discussion.

Because this is true, you may feel some apprehension about your ability to respond and to teach. You may not feel the same self-assurance you have in other teaching situations. Two things may help you: your willingness to be a model and your familiarity with the tools that are presented in the course–in particular, the Happiness List and I-Did-It List, and the methods for talking things over with yourself (see pages 46 – 47, 55 – 56, and 64 – 65).

We have found that teachers who are willing to be a model for the students by sharing their own experiences and feelings are more effective as facilitators and come away from the experience feeling that something significant has happened for everyone. This means that you let the students see that you, too, have situations in your life which require you to sort through your feelings, figure out which needs are important to meet at the time, and so on. This does not mean that you necessarily share in every activity. But whenever you see an opportunity to help students understand, by sharing a personal experience or feeling, do it.

"Your Role in Leading Discussions" on pages 6 – 7 will give you additional help in preparing yourself for this course.

Using the "Getting Personal" Activities in the Student's Book . . . .

Throughout *Stick Up For Yourself*, the student's book for this course, there are activities titled "Getting Personal." They can be used as optional activities for the students. Or you might decide to assign them, when assigning the students' reading for each session. Either way, let the students know, when writing is a part of the assignment, that what they write will be confidential. It should always be a student's decision whether or not to share what is written.

Encourage students to think of the "Getting Personal" activities as things that they can do now and might even want to do again after the course is finished. Point out that their ideas and feelings will be changing, and they may find they have new things to write about.

At minimum, ask them to read page xii in *Stick Up For Yourself*, to learn more about the reason for doing the "Getting Personal" activities.

GETTING READY

Informing and Involving Parents . . . .

Before you begin the course, send a letter to parents describing the course and telling them when it will start. Ask for their support and, if necessary, their written permission. A sample letter is found on page 97 in the Appendix. Be sure to send the letter at least one full week in advance.

Encourage parents to read the book for the course, *Stick Up For Yourself! Every Kid's Guide to Personal Power and Positive Self-Esteem*, by Gershen Kaufman, Ph.D. and Lev Raphael, Ph.D. Tell the students that their parents may be asking to borrow the book to read, and encourage them to take it home with them. If parents want to look at the book before the course begins, arrange for them to see a copy.

Mention to parents that their children want them to *know about* the course, but they may not always want to *talk about* it while they are taking it. Suggest that parents allow the students to bring it up.

Tell parents to feel free to call you with any questions they have, both before the course begins and during the course, and give them your phone number and convenient times to talk.

If you are teaching a group that is new to you, you may want to ask parents if there is anything they would like you to know about their children before the class begins.

At the end of the course, you may want to send parents an evaluation form, like the one found on page 110 in the Appendix, asking them about their perceptions of changes that have been taking place, and encouraging their comments.

Preparing the Room . . . .

The physical setting is important to the success of the course. If possible, schedule the sessions at a time when you will be as free of outside interruptions as possible. For example, try to avoid holding the sessions during a period of the day in which class members are regularly called out of the room for various reasons. It is frustrating to get the students involved and interested in the session and then have interruptions. In addition, when feelings are being shared it is disruptive to have people coming in and out who are not part of the group and are not aware of its discussion guidelines.

Think about how to organize the room for the session so that you can, if possible, be in a circle for group discussions. Allow space between any small groups, but keep it organized so that you are able to have a sense of what is going on in all the groups.

Think about how you might signal the beginning of the session. Turning the lights off and on is one way to get your students' attention. You might play a relaxing tape or record each time to let them know it is time to begin. Whatever you choose, you want it to be a pleasant way to shift gears.

Students' Guidelines for Discussions . . . .

Make clear at the first session the guidelines for discussion during group time. Here are some suggestions:

1. State that what is said in the group stays in the group, unless they have the permission of the person to talk about it.

2. Encourage students to listen, *really* listen to each other. This means that they are listening carefully, not planning what they are going to say when it is their turn.

3. Tell students that there are no right or wrong answers.

4. Sometimes students will want to share their thoughts and feelings; sometimes they won't. Let them know it is okay not to share. They can say, "I pass." At the same time, encourage sharing whenever it is comfortable to do so, because sharing allows feedback and support from the group. Point out that we also learn a lot by listening.

5. It's important to try to give everyone who wants to share an opportunity to do so. But sometimes you will need to move on before a student has said everything he or she wants to. When this happens, say, "I will come back to you if there is time."

Your Role in Leading Discussions . . . .

1. As teacher, you provide the structure. Be clear about the purpose of the session, and let the students know that it is your role to keep the session moving along.

2. Be a model for the students by being supportive and encouraging when they are talking.

3. Let them know you won't be judging what they say. Sometimes you may point out choices they have, but you won't be telling them which choice they *should* make or what they *should* think.

4. Make a point not to talk too much; you want all the class members to participate. When you have something to say, make it short and to the point, then reinvolve the students in the discussion.

5. Ask open-ended questions–not those that can be answered with a yes or no. You might ask, for example, "How would you feel if ...?" rather than "Would you be upset if ...?"

6. If you want to bring up a personal experience without identifying it as yours, you can begin by saying, "I have a friend who ...."

7. If someone is monopolizing discussion time, direct the attention away. You might say, for example, "Thank you for sharing. Now let's hear what other group members are thinking."

8. Be encouraging. Notice even small ways the students are learning and growing, and comment on them.

9. Find ways to involve everyone. If you have a student who is not ready to participate in discussions, find another role for him or her. Let the student hand out papers or arrange chairs, or ask the student to help you remember to do something.

10. It helps to see life–yours and theirs–as a great big journey. What you see and hear and learn along the way *is amazing.* If you can communicate that to your students, it may help them accept the process of change as a very natural, desirable thing.

Child Protection Laws . . . .

You need to understand that even though you talk to your group about confidentiality–what is said in the group stays in the group– there are certain things that you may hear or observe that you must report for the protection of the child and any others involved.

Before you teach the course, be absolutely clear that you know what you are legally required to report and what the guidelines for reporting are. These reporting requirements usually fall under the category of child protection legislation.

Most school districts and youth organizations have developed guidelines to conform to child protection laws. Find out what those guidelines are and who you need to report to, if the need arises.

Getting Support for Yourself . . . .

In a course such as this, in which feelings are expressed openly, you cannot anticipate what a session will be like or what needs may be revealed. There may be times when something happens in a session that you feel requires some follow-up, but you are not sure how to proceed. You may, for example, suspect that a child is showing signs of depression, but you're not sure if your hunch is accurate. You may notice that one student seems to have a great deal of anxiety. You may wonder, based on what a student is sharing in the group, whether there is a need for counseling or some follow-up to the group experience. You may not know what to do about a student who tends to be disruptive, but only in small group situations.

To help you debrief after a session, you may want to prearrange with someone the option of taking time to talk about what went on in a session–a school counselor, the school psychologist, or another teacher who has led similar classes. Know in advance who can give you this support. You can talk about what went on, but you will want to take care to follow the confidentiality guidelines, just as the students do.

For an additional discussion of the principles presented in this course, you may want to read *Dynamics of Power: Building a Competent Self*, by Gershen Kaufman and Lev Raphael. See "Resources," page 113, for information.

Relating Activities to Your Group . . . .

Many of the activities in this course revolve around students' discussion of their own life experiences. This has a side benefit of automatically relating the course to the community you are in.

If students can't relate to an activity, they will be unable to use it as a springboard, and the discussion may fall flat. Often a minor change is all that is needed to help them relate the activity to their lives. It is a good idea to read through all the activities for a session before you conduct the session; if you feel that particular activities are not relevant to your community, alter them to fit your needs.

SESSIONS

Session 1

What Does it Mean to Stick Up for Yourself?

Overview

This session introduces the course. Students learn what "stick up for yourself" means. In short, students discover that it doesn't mean getting back at someone else, being bossy or stuck up, or saying and doing whatever they want, wherever they want. It does mean being true to yourself, speaking up for yourself when it is appropriate, and sticking up for yourself with yourself. Students are introduced to the idea that the two things they need in order to stick up for themselves are *personal power* and *positive self-esteem*. Throughout the course they will be learning how to develop these two important ideas.

Before the First Session

Before the course begins, tell students they will need to bring a notebook to the first session.

Make copies of the list of session topics and reading assignments to hand out to each class member and to post on the reading table (if students are sharing copies of *Stick Up For Yourself*). You may want to reproduce the list found in the Appendix on page 98, adding dates or other information about location and times as needed.

To honor the class members' right to privacy, begin right away developing the understanding that there will be times they choose to participate and times they choose to listen; either response is okay.

You may have already established guidelines for discussions; if so, a brief reminder may be all that is necessary. If, however, you have not worked with this class before, or if there are new members who may not be familiar with the guidelines, plan to spend time during the first session going over them. (See "Students' Guidelines for Discussions," page 6.) Be certain class members understand that they have a right to choose to participate, to the degree they feel comfortable.

If you choose to follow our recommendation that you send a letter to the parents detailing the course objectives, be sure to send it at least one week in advance to allow time for parents' questions to be answered. A sample letter is found on page 97 in the Appendix.

Learner Outcomes_____

The purpose of this session is to help class members:

■ Prepare for the course.

■ Become familiar with the phrase "stick up for yourself" as it is used in this course.

■ Identify situations in which they feel they need to learn new ways to stick up for themselves.

Materials_____

■ A list of session topics for each student (optional); a reproducible copy of the session topics and reading assignments is in the Appendix on page 98. (Activity 1)

■ A chalkboard or flip chart. (Activities 2, 4, 6)

■ Copies of the student's book, *Stick Up For Yourself*. (Activity 3)

■ A blank piece of paper for each student. (Activity 5)

■ A notebook for each student. (Activity 6)

Agenda_____

1. Orient students to the course.

2. Ask students to brainstorm what it means to stick up for yourself.

3. Allow students time for reading pages ix – xi in *Stick Up For Yourself*.

4. Reexamine the list students made when brainstorming (Activity 2) to see if their reading changed their ideas about what it means to stick up for yourself.

5. Lead the activity, "Mix Up," in which situations and ways to stick up for yourself are randomly, and sometimes humorously, matched.

6. Ask students to identify and write down their goals for the course.

7. Close the session with a brief statement about what was discussed, and assign the reading for the next session.

Activities_____

1. Orientation

- Tell class members:

— *When you are finished with this course, you will have a better understanding of what it means to stick up for yourself.*

— *You will learn about things you can do–right now and in the future–to stick up for yourself.*

— *You will be asked to do some reading and to keep a notebook. Have the notebook with you at each session.*

— *You are encouraged to take part in all the activities. Sometimes that will mean you choose to share your ideas and thoughts, other times it may just mean being here and listening.*

— *In this course, we will often spend time listening to each other; showing respect for each other is very important.*

(**Note**: If you feel your class needs specifics about what it means to listen respectfully to others, take a minute to go over those now.)

— *You will be evaluating yourself at the end of the course.*

- (**Optional**) Hand out the list of session topics and reading assignments found on page 98 in the Appendix.

2. What Does "Stick Up for Yourself" Mean?

- Ask class members:

— *What do you think it means to stick up for yourself?*

- Write their ideas on a chalkboard or flip chart, without commenting or asking for clarification.

3. Reading

- Ask them to read pages ix – xi in *Stick Up For Yourself*. Tell them to close their books when they're done so you'll be able to tell they're ready to go on.

4. What Does "Stick Up for Yourself" Mean? (continued)

- Go back to the list they brainstormed before reading (Activity 2). Ask class members:

  — *After reading, you may have changed your mind about what it means to stick up for yourself. Let's look at the list we made earlier.*

  — *Now we know that sticking up for yourself doesn't mean getting back at someone else. Is there anything on our list that we might want to change? Anything that might suggest we want revenge rather than to stick up for ourselves?*

  — *Sticking up for yourself doesn't mean acting bossy or stuck-up. Is there anything on this list that we might want to change?*

  — *Speaking up for yourself is one way to stick up for yourself; did we have that on our list?*

  — *What about being true to yourself? Is there anything here about being true to yourself, which is a way we stick up for ourselves?*

5. Mix Up

- Hand out a small blank piece of paper to each class member. (It needs to be large enough to hold one sentence.)

- Count off by 3's (1, 2, 3, 1, 2, 3, and so on) until each member of the class has a number.

- Ask the students who are 1's to raise their hands. Say:

  — *Think of a name of a popular actor or actress or a cartoon character. Write the name on your paper.*

- Ask the students who are 2's to raise their hands. Say:

  — *Think of a situation you might get into at home, at school, or at a friend's house, in which you might have to stick up for yourself. Write it on your paper.*

- Brainstorm with the 2's for a minute if they need help. Here are ideas:

  Your older brother borrowed your favorite tape without asking.

  Your teacher lost your homework assignment and gave you a zero.

Your mom forgot to pick you up after football practice.

The bus driver threw you off the bus because he thought you were shoving and pushing.

- ■ Ask the students who are 3's to raise their hands. Say:

— *Think of a way you would stick up for yourself. Write it on your paper.*

(Show the 3's the list the class made up earlier, in Activity 2, if they need help.)

- ■ Now ask the students to get into groups; each group should have a 1, a 2, and a 3. Say:

— *Now we'll go around the room giving each group a turn. You'll each read what is on your paper. #1 reads the name of the character, #2 tells us the situation the character is in, and #3 tells us what the character will do. Just read what's on your paper, starting with #1. Do it quickly. Ready? Let's go.*

- ■ Conclude the activity by saying:

— *Sometimes what we do to stick up for ourselves works; sometimes it doesn't.*

— *Sometimes we are hooked into ideas of how to stick up for ourselves and aren't aware of other ways. Sometimes we notice how other people stick up for themselves.*

— *Sticking up for yourself is not always something other people can see or hear.*

6. Goal Setting

- ■ Write the following on the chalkboard or flip chart:

  In this course, I want to learn new ways to stick up for myself when . . .

- ■ Hand out notebooks (or ask participants to take out the notebooks they brought with them for the course).

■ Say:

— *Copy what I have written here into your notebook. Then take a few minutes to finish the sentence. At the end of the course, you'll have a chance to look back at what you write today to see if you have learned what you hoped to learn.*

7. Session Closing

■ Write the following on the chalkboard or flip chart:

Personal power (knowing who you are)
Positive self-esteem (liking yourself)

■ Summarize by saying:

— *In this course, you will learn what it means to stick up for yourself. These two things–personal power and positive self-esteem–will help you stick up for yourself, wherever you are, whatever situation you are in.*

— *In the next session, we'll begin talking about personal power.*

— *Before the next session, please read pages 1 – 7 and 61 – 63 in* Stick Up For Yourself.

■ If necessary, tell students where and when the next session will be.

Session 2

You Are Responsible for Your Behavior and Feelings

Overview_____

In this session, personal power is defined as "being secure and confident within yourself." Personal power is presented as something which can be developed by everyone. Students learn that personal power has four parts: being responsible for your behavior and feelings, making choices, getting to know yourself, and getting and using power in your relationships and your life.

This session is devoted to the first part–being responsible for your behavior and feelings. Students learn that even though other people may sometimes do or say things that we respond to with a certain feeling or behavior, they did not make us do it. Similarly, even though other people respond to what we say or do in a certain way, we did not make them feel or behave that way. Each of us is responsible for our own behavior and feelings. At the same time, students learn that being responsible isn't the same as being perfect.

One of the principal tools used in the course, the Happiness List, is introduced as a powerful way to begin storing and collecting good feelings, which, in turn, helps us develop personal power and positive self-esteem.

Learner Outcomes_____

The purpose of this session is to help class members:

- Identify that being responsible for their feelings and behavior is one way to develop personal power.

- Identify that any time they claim "you made me do it" as a way of explaining their feelings and behavior, they are avoiding being responsible.

- Identify that what others do might "trigger" a feeling or behavior, but it does not mean that others are responsible for their (the students') feelings or behavior.

- Understand that they are responsible for their own feelings and behavior.

- Discover one new way to stick up for themselves when they make mistakes.

- Identify the Happiness List as a way to begin collecting and storing good feelings to help them develop personal power.

Materials

- An object that illustrates a wall or barrier; a sign that says "You Made Me Do It!" (Activity 2)

- A list of questions to hand out during role play (Activity 2); a reproducible list is found on page 99 in the Appendix.

- The student's book, *Stick Up For Yourself.* (Activities 3, 6)

- A chalkboard or flip chart. (Activity 5)

- A notebook for each class member. (Activities 5, 6)

- A copy for each student of "Keeping Your Happiness List"; (a reproducible copy is on page 100 in the Appendix). (Activity 6)

Agenda

1. Introduce the session.

2. Lead the role play, "You Made Me Do It."

3. Allow time for reading (if they haven't already done so) and discussing pages 1 – 7 in *Stick Up For Yourself.*

4. Lead a discussion about how other people "trigger" our reactions.

5. Lead the activity, "Nobody's Perfect," and ask students to write at least one new way they will deal with their mistakes.

6. Explain "The Happiness List." Give students time to write their happiness lists for today, and spend time discussing their reactions.

7. Close with a brief statement about what was discussed and what the next session will be about, then assign the reading for the next session.

Activities_____

1. Introduction

- ■ Tell students:

- — *Today you'll learn more about how to stick up for yourself. One way to stick up for yourself is by getting and using personal power. Being responsible is an important part of personal power.*

- — *Being responsible doesn't mean carrying the whole world on your shoulders like Atlas–but it is a big job! In this session you will be learning about what you are responsible for–your feelings and behavior.*

2. Role Play: "You Made Me Do It"

- ■ Ask group members:

- — *Has your doctor ever taken a little hammer-like instrument and tapped it on the front part of your knee? What happened?*

- — *Did you make your knee jerk, or did it just happen?*

- — *We call that an automatic response. When someone does something without thinking, it might be described as a "knee-jerk response." For a few minutes, we're going to talk about words many of us automatically say when something goes wrong and we don't want to be seen as the one responsible–"You made me do it!"*

- — *Unfortunately, those words may be a signal that we're not being responsible for our behavior and feelings.*

- ■ Show group members an object in the room that suggests a barrier or wall. Place the sign on it which says, "You Made Me Do It."

- ■ Tell class members:

- — *The words "You made me do it" are sometimes a wall we put up. We may do this automatically, like the knee-jerk response, or we may do it only now and then. Either way, whenever we say "You made me do it," it is a sign that we are not being responsible for our behavior and feelings.*

- ■ Tell class members:

- — *For fun, you're going to role-play in pairs. One person will ask a question. The other person will answer the question with what we are going to call a "You-made-me-do-it" answer.*

You won't use the words, "You made me do it," but that's the message you want to get across.

— *Here's an example:*

— *The question is: "Why didn't you take out the garbage?"*

— *A "you-made-me-do-it" answer is: "You didn't put it by the back door, so I didn't know it needed to go out."*

— *Can you think of another "you-made-me-do-it" answer for this question?*

■ If they can't think of one, you might want to use one or more of the following:

— *"You didn't tell me it was full."*

— *"You never said that was my job this week."*

— *"You didn't sort the stuff for recycling."*

— *"You didn't get me up early enough, so I didn't have time."*

■ When you are sure the class has the idea, divide them into pairs (or into groups of three or four people, if that works better).

■ Hand out the list of questions that are shown below; there is a reproducible list on page 99 in the Appendix.

Where is your homework?

Why didn't you call like you said you would?

Why did you wear my sweater without asking?

Who told you that you could do that?

What happened to the change?

Why are you late?

Why aren't the dishes washed?

Who broke this?

Tell me why your grades dropped.

■ Ask the students to try to think of at least one you-made-me-do-it answer for each question. Tell them they'll only have a few minutes, so they need to do it fast. They can skip a question if they're having trouble thinking of an answer.

- Bring the groups back together again, but have them stay in the same area with their small group. Ask one of the questions. Go from group to group asking them to quickly give one answer they came up with in their group.

- Comment (if it's appropriate) that it didn't seem hard for them to come up with answers, and say that you wonder if that means they're experts.

- End the activity by saying:

— *Being responsible for your feelings and behavior can help you get and use personal power.*

— *At one time or another, you may catch yourself saying to someone, "You made me do it!"*

— *Saying "You made me do it" is a way we avoid being responsible. It is a wall we put up that keeps us from getting and using personal power.*

— *Whenever you hear yourself saying "You made me do it," remind yourself: "No one else is responsible for my behavior or feelings; no one made me do it."*

3. Reading (or Reviewing Your Reading Assignment)

- If your class did not have an opportunity to read pages 1 – 7 before the session, give them time now.

- Ask the class:

— *If someone talks you into doing something, are you responsible for your behavior?*

— *If you do something without thinking—you just do it—are you responsible? Why or why not? When has this happened to you?*

— *If you do something which you really didn't mean to do, are you responsible? Why or why not? When has this happened to you?*

— *Can someone else make you feel angry or sad or happy? Why or why not? (What someone else says may "trigger" your feelings, but they didn't make you feel that way. You are responsible for your own feelings.)*

— *On page 6, find what the authors say is the main reason for being responsible. When you find it, raise your hand.*

(Ask someone to read aloud what they found: "The main reason is because it's the best thing to do for you. It helps you feel secure and confident inside yourself. It gives you a feeling of personal power.")

- ■ Tell the class:

— *It may take time before you are really comfortable with the fact that you are responsible for your own behavior and feelings.*

— *Change takes time.*

— *Changing the way you think about things is like wearing a new pair of shoes. Sometimes it takes awhile before new shoes are comfortable to walk in. They may even pinch your feet. If you keep wearing them, they start to feel more comfortable and natural–a part of you.*

— *Keep in mind that being responsible is a way to get and use personal power.*

4. Triggers

- ■ Ask the class:

— *Have you ever said to someone, "I knew you would say that!" or, "I knew you would do that!" Can you give me an example?*

— *How did you know what they were going to do or say?*

(Lead the discussion until someone expresses the idea that we know what they are going to do or say because we've seen them react that way in similar situations.)

— *How many of you know something you could say to someone, and then they would cry or get angry? Why do you feel so sure about that?*

(You are leading the discussion to help them see that we begin to predict someone's behavior because (1) we've seen them react in a similar situation, and (2) we know what is important to them.)

— *Even though you are responsible only for your own behavior, sometimes your behavior might "trigger" a behavior or feeling in another person.*

— *Here are two examples:*

You didn't make *your friend cry. But when you didn't ask her to your party, she felt sad. Not getting an invitation was a trigger for her sadness.*

Your brother didn't make *you angry. But when he spilled paint on your new shirt, it was a trigger for your anger.*

- Ask the class:

— *If your mom always gets angry when you leave dirty dishes on the floor in your room, are you responsible for her feeling angry?* (No)

— *Were the dirty dishes a trigger?*

— *Do you think that leaving the dirty dishes on the floor would be a trigger if you had never done this before? Is it more likely to be a trigger if you have done it many times before?*

- Tell everyone to pair up with a person nearby.

- Say:

— *Take turns. First tell about something you do that triggers a feeling or behavior in someone else. Then tell about something someone else does that triggers a reaction in you. First, something you do. Then something someone else does.*

- After two or three minutes, bring the class back together and ask:

— *Would anyone like to share what you do that triggers a reaction in someone else?*

— *Did anyone think of something that someone else does that triggers an angry feeling in you? A hurt feeling? A happy feeling? An excited feeling? A scared feeling? An ashamed feeling?*

— *Can you think of one way that being aware of triggers can help you?*

5. Nobody's Perfect

- Ask the class:

— *Has anyone here ever made a mistake?*

— *Raise your hand if you've made one mistake.*

— *Is there anyone who has made two? Three? More than three? More than you can count?*

— *Who is the Mistake Champion of the World? I'm sure I've got you beat. You haven't lived as long as I have.*

— *Now is there anyone here who thinks they're never going to make another mistake?*

— *Who would like to think they're not going to make the same mistakes?*

- Tell the class:

— *You're going to make mistakes. It's part of life.*

— *When you do, being responsible means you don't immediately try to find someone else to blame.*

— *What you tell yourself, and how you feel after you make a mistake, are important to your self-esteem.*

— *You need to learn to keep liking yourself, even when you make a mistake.*

- Ask the class:

— *What do you tell yourself when you make a mistake?*

— *Do you know what it means to forgive yourself?*

- Write the following on the chalkboard or flip chart:

When I make a mistake, I usually tell myself . . .
From now on, when I make a mistake I'm going to tell myself . . .

- Ask students to open their notebooks.

- Say:

— *In your notebook, copy and finish the sentences I've written here.*

6. The Happiness List

- Tell the class members:

— *Turn to a clean page in your notebook.*

- Ask:

— *Has anybody ever told you that you are a collector? What did they mean?*

- Tell the class:

— *Some people collect lots and lots of things, and the spaces where they live or work or go to school become packed with things. We do this with feelings, too. We collect feelings. And those collected feelings become part of a bigger and bigger collection.*

— *It's important to have good feelings in your collection.*

— *Remembering good feelings is one way you help yourself feel secure and confident, no matter what!*

— *Collecting and storing feelings can help you get and use personal power–if your collection is made up of good feelings.*

■ Tell the class:

— *Pages 62 and 63 in your book talk about the Happiness List. Turn to the bottom of page 62 and read along as I read the five reasons it is so important to keep a Happiness List every day.*

"1. It boosts your *personal power.*

2. It teaches you that *you are responsible* for your own happiness.

3. It teaches you that *you can choose* how to experience your life.

4. It teaches you to look for things which *create* happiness.

5. It teaches you how to *collect and store* good feelings."

■ Tell the class:

— *Today we are going to start keeping a Happiness List, and we'll do this for the rest of the course. Or maybe for the rest of our lives! Who knows–maybe we could end up with the biggest collection of good feelings in the history of the world!*

— *These don't have to be "Big Things." Noticing small things can make us happy, too. Start to notice what makes you smile. Those may be things you want to put on your list. Let's get started.*

— *Right now, write down five things that happened today which you feel good about, which put a smile on your face.*

■ Ask students:

— *Did you find this easy to do, or was it difficult? Does anyone want to tell how they felt about doing this?*

— *Anyone else?*

■ Tell students:

— *Here are six things to do to help you get the most from your Happiness List.*

■ Hand out "Keeping Your Happiness List" (a reproducible copy is on page 100 in the Appendix). Read it to the students or ask them to read:

1. Notice the event when it occurs.
2. Feel the good feeling.

3. Collect and store it inside you.
4. Write it down on your list.
5. Review your list at the end of the day.
6. Feel the good feelings all over again.

■ Conclude the activity by saying:

— *For the rest of the course, keep a Happiness List every day. Do it every day. Start your collection and watch it grow.*

— *In future sessions, we'll talk more about the Happiness List. For now, just get started.*

7. Session Closing

■ Summarize by saying:

— *In this session, we learned that we are responsible for our behavior and feelings. We are not responsible for other people's feelings or behavior, only our own.*

— *One way to be more responsible is to stop saying, "You made me do it."*

— *We also learned about triggers. Sometimes our behavior triggers certain feelings or behaviors in other people. But we didn't make them do it. They are responsible for their behavior and feelings. just as we are responsible for our own.*

— *Sometimes other people's behavior triggers certain feelings or reactions in us, but they didn't make us do it! We are responsible for our behavior and feelings, just as they are responsible for their own behavior and feelings.*

— *Everyone makes mistakes. It is important to expect to make mistakes at least four times every day. It is also important to forgive ourselves when we make mistakes.*

— *One way to get and use personal power is to collect good feelings. Keeping a Happiness List will help us do that.*

— *In the next session, we'll begin talking about another important part of developing personal power: choices.*

■ Tell students:

— *Before the next session, read pages 8 – 13 in* Stick Up For Yourself.

■ If necessary, tell students where and when the next session will be.

Session 3

Making Choices

Overview

In this session, students develop an understanding of the statement, "Because you are responsible for your behavior and feelings, you can make choices about them."

Students learn the importance of identifying and making choices. Activities help them learn to separate "feeling" from "acting on feelings." Although they have some choices regarding how they feel, they have more choices in what to do about the feeling.

The relationship between expectations and feelings is discussed. To determine what their expectations are, they can learn to ask, "What do I hope will happen? What are the chances it will happen?" Having realistic expectations helps them develop personal power.

Learner Outcomes

The purpose of this session is to help class members:

- Understand that they can choose how to feel.

- Understand that they can choose what to do about a feeling.

- Identify realistic and unrealistic expectations.

- Identify ways that their feelings and their expectations are sometimes tied together.

Materials

- The student's book, *Stick Up For Yourself.* (Activity 2)

- A chalkboard or flip chart. (Activity 4)

- Students' notebooks. (Activity 5)

Agenda

1. Introduce the session.

2. Allow students time to read pages 8 – 13 in *Stick Up For Yourself*, and have a brief discussion.

3. Lead the activity, "Choices."
   Optional: Conclude this activity with a role play.

4. Lead the activity, "What Do You Expect?" to help students identify realistic and unrealistic expectations.

5. Lead the activity, "Becoming More Realistic," to develop students' understanding of how expectations influence feelings.

6. Close with a brief summary of what was discussed, and assign the reading for the next session.

Activities

1. Introduction

- Tell the class:

  — *This session is about choices you can make in how you feel and act.*

  — *How many of you often say or think, "I had no choice"?*

  — *Sometimes you're right; you don't* **always** *have a choice about something you have to do. But sometimes you overlook choices. This session will help you begin to notice the choices you have.*

  — *Identifying choices and making good ones are things you can do to stick up for yourself.*

2. Reading

- Ask the class to read pages 8 – 13 in their books. Tell them to close their books when they're done so that you'll be able to tell they're ready to go on.

- Say to the students:

  — *In our textbook, you read about Sara, who got a paper back from her teacher. The teacher had written, "You can do better." Imagine yourself in that situation for a minute. How would you feel?*

— *Sara could be angry or sad. Or, as the authors point out, she could decide that what she did was good enough. That is a way to stick up for yourself.*

— *Who has had an experience like Larry–you need to talk to someone right away and you can't get the person's attention for one reason or another? How did you feel? Why do you think you felt that way? What did you do? What else could you have done?*

— *Being able to identify choices we have about our feelings and our actions gives us personal power.*

3. Choices

■ Tell the class:

— *We're going to take a few minutes to listen to a story and practice identifying possible choices that a boy named Joseph has.*

■ Ask the class to listen as you read (you may need to read the story more than once):

— *Joseph is at a friend's apartment. He has to be home by 10 p.m. To catch a subway that will get him home by 10:00, he has to leave his friend's apartment by 9:30. He misses the train. The next train will come at 9:45, and he'll be home at 10:15. But he isn't supposed to ride the subway after 9:30. If he takes the bus, he won't get home until 10:30. He is supposed to call his mother if he is going to take the bus instead of the subway. But if he takes time to call her now, he'll miss the bus.*

■ Stop the story and ask:

— *What choices does Joseph have?*

(Allow time for discussion. Class members may pick up on the fact that regardless of what Joseph decides to do, he's going to break one of his mom's "rules"–he's either going to take the subway later than he's supposed to, or he's going to take the bus but not have time to call his mother first like he's supposed to.)

■ Continue the story:

— *If he takes the bus, he'll be a half hour late. He decides it would be better to be only fifteen minutes late by riding the subway than to be a half hour late by riding the bus. And, if he rides the bus, he doesn't have time to call his mother to let her know.*

- Stop the story and ask:

— *What do you think of the choice Joseph made? Why?*

- Continue the story:

— *When he is coming out of the subway station, he looks up and sees his mom waiting at the top of the stairs.*

- Stop the story and ask:

-- *What choices does he have now? In what he feels? In how he acts?*

- Continue the story:

— *The first thing his mom says to him is, "I told you not to ride the subway after 9:30."*

- Ask:

— *What do you think Joseph is feeling right now?*

— *What choices does he have right now in how he feels or acts?*

— *What could he say or do that might help the situation?*

— *What could he say or do that would make the situation worse?*

   (**Note:** You may either conclude the activity at this point, or go on and do a brief role play, using volunteers.)

- If you are ending the activity now, conclude by saying:

— *We can't always predict what choices we're going to have to make. Sometimes we make good choices, sometimes not so good.*

— *We gain personal power when we learn to recognize–on the spot– the choices that are ours to make.*

Optional Role Play

- Ask:

— *Has anybody here ever come home later than you were supposed to?*

- Ask the class to divide into pairs.

- In each pair, ask the person whose first name begins with the letter that is closest to the front of the alphabet to play the role of the parent, and ask the other person to play the role of the child.

- Say:

  — *Here is the situation: If you are the child, you are just walking into your home. You are an hour late, and your parent is waiting for you.*

- Say:

  — *Take a couple of minutes to decide two things: (1) how you're going to act, and (2) how you're going to let us know what you're feeling.*

- Bring the class back together and ask for volunteers to begin the role play.

- Ask the class:

  — *Did you have any trouble figuring out what each person was feeling?*

  — *Was there a place where either of them seemed to make a choice?*

- Ask for volunteers for one more role play.

- Say:

  — *This time, without using words, I want you to act out the scene.*

- Ask the class:

  — *Did you have any trouble figuring out what they were feeling?*

- Conclude by saying:

  — *We have choices in how we act and how we feel.*

  — *We gain personal power when we learn to recognize–on the spot– the choices that are ours to make.*

4. What Do You Expect?

- Say to the class:

  — *Sometimes we set ourselves up for disappointment. One way we do it is this: we hope something will happen that is not likely to happen.*

- Write this sentence on the chalkboard or flip chart:
  Rx for Disappointment:
  We hope something will happen that is not likely to happen.

  — *When we don't get what we hoped for, we may become angry or sad. We might even feel that it is somehow our fault. In this activity, we're going to practice identifying the kinds of things we may hope for that set us up for disappointment.*

- Give this example:

— *What if I say to myself, "I'm going to smile at you more often because if I smile it will make you all feel very happy."*

— *What do I expect to happen because I smile? Do you think that is a realistic expectation? Is it likely to happen?* (No, it is unrealistic.)

— *What if I say, "I'm going to smile at you more often so that you will be able to see how much I enjoy being with you." Is that a realistic expectation? Is it likely that my smiling will let you know I like being with you?*

- Choose three of the following sentences (or others that you feel may be more relevant to your group), and write them on the chalkboard or flip chart:

  If I lose ten pounds, ...
  If I gain ten pounds, ...
  If I get in with the right group, ...
  If I change my hairdo, ...
  If I grow two inches taller, ...
  When I leave home, ...
  When I have a boyfriend (girlfriend), my life will be ...
  If I go to a different school next year, ...

- Divide the class into small groups, with 2 or 3 persons in each group.

- Tell them that each group will make up endings for the sentences on the board–but some groups will do realistic endings, and others will do unrealistic ones.

- Go around to each group and whisper to them whether they are to make up realistic or unrealistic endings.

- After a few minutes, bring them back together. Read the first sentence. Ask one of the small groups to read aloud the ending they wrote.

- Ask the rest of the class:

— *Was that a realistic or unrealistic ending? Why do you think so?*

  (The unrealistic endings should be obvious. Some of the realistic endings may seem debatable, and you will need to allow some discussion. Move on before the discussion begins to drag.)

- Continue until you have given each small group at least one opportunity.

- End the activity when it is clear that the class understands the difference between realistic and unrealistic expectations.

- Ask:

— *Who can summarize for us how realistic expectations affect feelings?*

5. Becoming More Realistic

- Tell them:

-- *I want you to think of something that happens in your life that always makes you feel angry or sad. Think about that feeling for a minute.*

- Say:

— *In your notebook, finish these sentences, describing the feeling you're thinking about right now.*

  I think I feel that way because . . .
  What I always hope will happen is . . .
  The chances it will happen are . . .

- Tell them:

-- *Now I want you to think of something that happens in your life that always makes you feel happy. Think about that feeling for a minute.*

- Say:

— *In your notebook, finish these sentences, describing the feeling you're thinking about right now.*

  I think I feel that way because . . .
  What I always hope will happen is . . .
  The chances it will happen are . . .

- Ask:

— *In the situation you wrote about, is it possible that your feelings had a lot to do with what you hoped or expected would happen?*

— *Would anyone like to share his or her thoughts with us?*

- Conclude by saying:

  During this week, try to be aware of times you feel angry or sad. When it happens, ask yourself, "What was I expecting?" This may help you figure out whether or not you have realistic expectations for yourself and other people.

6. Session Closing

- Summarize by saying:

— *In this session, you learned that part of sticking up for yourself is making choices–on the spot–about how to feel or act.*

— *Sometimes you may feel disappointed or angry or sad because your expectations are not realistic.*

— *Having realistic expectations can help you develop more personal power.*

- Tell class members:

— *Before the next session, please read pages 14 – 31 in* Stick Up For Yourself. *Next week, we'll be talking about feelings, and we'll be learning how to give them names.*

- If necessary, tell students where and when the next session will be.

Session 4 Naming Your Feelings

Overview

This session is designed to help class members learn to name their feelings. Students learn that one part of getting to know themselves is learning to call feelings by their right names. This is a vital session because students' personal power is very often dependent on whether or not they are able to name (and then claim or own) the feeling they are having. Activities and discussion develop the understanding that the body's reaction helps us identify a feeling.

Learner Outcomes

The purpose of this session is to help group members:

■ Understand that part of sticking up for themselves is knowing what they are feeling.

■ Identify and name feelings.

■ Understand that knowing names for feelings makes it easier to accurately communicate what they are feeling.

Materials

■ The student's book, *Stick Up For Yourself.* (Activities 2, 3)

■ Slips of paper with the name of one *low-intensity* feeling written on each. (See page 17 of student text.) (Activity 3)

■ Chalkboard or flip chart. (Activity 4)

■ Students' notebooks. (Activity 5)

Agenda

1. Introduce the session.

2. Review one part of the reading assignment, and tell how the reading will be used in this session.

3. Lead the role-play activity, "Name That Feeling."

4. Lead the discussion, "What Your Body Is Telling You," to help group members learn to notice how their bodies can help them name their feelings.

5. Lead the activity, "Recipe for a Feeling," to help group members identify "ingredients" that might result in a certain feeling.

6. Close the session and give the reading assignment.

Activities_____

1. Introduction

- Tell group members:

— *In earlier sessions we learned two ways to get personal power: (1) being responsible for your feelings and behavior, and (2) making choices.*

— *Today we're going to begin talking about a third way to get personal power: getting to know yourself. An important part of knowing yourself is knowing what you are feeling. This session is about naming your feelings.*

2. Reading

- Ask the group to turn to page 15 in *Stick Up For Yourself*. Tell them to read silently, while you read the last three paragraphs:

"Feelings have their own special names. The more names you know, the more you can understand your feelings and tell other people about them. And the more you can stick up for yourself.

"Names are like 'handles' for our feelings. Knowing the right name for a feeling allows us to 'pick it up,' learn about it, and make choices about it.

"Calling feelings by their right names adds to your personal power. Calling feelings by their wrong names takes away from your personal power."

- Say to the group members:

— *We're not going to take time right now to read or review all the pages on feelings (pages 14 – 31). Instead, we'll be reading parts of it as we do the activities in this session.*

3. Name That Feeling

- Ask the group:

  — *Has anyone ever asked you, "How do you feel about what happened?" and you couldn't think of an answer?*

  — *Before we can tell someone about what we're feeling–or even describe it to ourselves–it helps to have a name for the feeling.*

- Say to the group:

  — *Turn to page 17. We're going to take a few minutes to talk about the eight low-intensity feelings that are listed at the bottom of the page.*

  — *Let's start with "Interested." I'd like someone to volunteer to read the first sentence on page 18, which tells about "Interested."*

- Follow this procedure until you have gone through the eight feelings on the low-intensity list: (Interested, Enjoying Yourself, Surprised, Distressed, Fearful, Angry, Ashamed, Contemptuous).

- Tell the group:

  — *We're going to do a role play. I'm going to divide you into small groups. Each group will get a slip of paper with a name of a feeling written on it from the list of feelings we just read about.*

- Tell the group:

  — *Your group has to figure out how to show us the feeling, by your behavior, not by words. Decide as a group whether everybody in the group will do the same thing, or if each of you will do something different. Remember, you can't tell us the name of the feeling; you have to show us.*

  — *If you can't figure out what to do, you might want to reread the part of your book that talks about that feeling.*

  — *Any questions? (Answer any questions they have.)*

- Divide into small groups. Give each group a slip of paper with the name of the feeling which they are to act out. (Assign the same feeling to more than one group.)

- After giving them time to practice, call the groups back together and point to one group to begin.

- After the group "shows" the feeling, ask the others:

  — *What feeling are they acting out?*

— *Why do you think so?*

— *What helped you decide? Was anything confusing?*

■ Take turns until each group has had a chance.

■ Conclude by saying:

— *In this activity, we practiced naming feelings based on what we saw. Nonverbal behavior helped us "read" and name feelings.*

4. What Your Body Is Telling You

■ Before you begin this activity, on a chalkboard or flip chart, write the names of the high-intensity feelings listed on page 17 of *Stick Up For Yourself:*

Excited
Joyful
Startled
Anguished
Terrified
Enraged
Humiliated
Disgusted

■ Say to the group:

— *You can learn a lot about your feelings by "listening" to what your body is telling you.*

— *Think about the last time you were really angry–enraged. How does it feel when you are enraged? Where in your body do you feel rage?*

(Write their answers beside "Enraged" on the list. Their answers might include: I clench my fists, I feel my face get hot, I feel like I need to scream.)

— *What about "Terrified"? How does your body help you know you are terrified?*

(Write their answers beside "Terrified" on the list. Their answers might include: I can't move (frozen stiff), I have a tight feeling in my stomach, I have cold hands, I am extra alert and watchful, I am nervous, my body is shaking, my knees are shaking, my teeth chatter.)

— *What about "Startled"? How does your body let you know you're startled?*

(Write their answers beside "Startled" on the list. Their answers might include: I yell out loud, I jump, I put my hands up to my chest, I protect my eyes with my hands.)

■ Continue until you have at least one or two bodily or facial reactions written beside each of the eight words on the list.

■ Conclude the activity by saying:

— *While you are learning to name your feelings, it is helpful to tune in to what your body is telling you. You experience the feeling not only in your mind but in your body, too. As you practice, you'll get better and better at naming your feelings.*

— *Remember, knowing what you are feeling can help you know what to do about the feeling.*

5. Recipe for a Feeling

■ Tell them:

— *For fun, let's make up a recipe for a feeling.*

— *We know the amounts of each ingredient, but we don't know what the ingredients are. Let's start with "joyful." The ingredients have to be something that might happen to bring about that feeling.*

(If they're having trouble getting the idea, you can suggest that you start out with a quart of "time off from school," or 1 tablespoon of "good jokes," or 1 cup of "sleepovers.")

■ You might want to show them one of the following, done by other students when they took the *Stick Up For Yourself* course.

"Excited"

Mix together:
3 cups enthusiasm
1/4 cup happy voices
1 tsp. great news
Add 2 tsp. of water
Add favorite verb
Stir
Bake at 350 degrees for 10 minutes.

"Joyful"

1 tsp. presents
1/2 T fun activities
2 T anything that makes you happy
1/4 tsp. water
1 party

■ Write the following parts of the recipe on the chalkboard or flip chart:

A "Joyful" Recipe

1/2 teaspoon of ...
1 cup of ...
2 Tablespoons of ...
1 quart of ...

■ Say:

— *Here is what we know so far.* (Point to the ingredients and read what you have written.)

— *Let's finish the recipe.*

(Write their suggestions on the board next to the ingredient.)

■ When the recipe is finished, have someone read it out loud.

■ Tell them:

— *Now I want you to take out your notebook and write a recipe for a different feeling–one that you would like to have more often. There is one rule for this: none of the ingredients should suggest violence.*

■ After giving them time to write, ask:

— *Does anyone have a recipe they'd like to share?*

— *Just read your ingredients. Let us see if we can figure out what the feeling is.*

■ Tell the group:

— *There is not just one recipe for a feeling. But this activity shows us that we know a lot about why we sometimes feel the way we do.*

- Conclude by saying:

— *During this week, try to be aware of times you are feeling something. Think about it for a few minutes. Ask yourself, "What was happening around me and inside me when I felt that way?" You might begin to see what makes you feel mad, or sad, or glad.*

6. Session Closing

- Summarize by saying:

— *In this session, you learned that naming your feelings is an important part of getting to know yourself.*

— *You learned that one way to name your feelings is to listen to what your body is telling you.*

— *When you are able to give your feeling the right name, you can choose what to do about it.*

- Tell group members:

— *Before the next session, please read pages 44 – 50 in* Stick Up For Yourself. *Next week, we'll be talking about what it means to claim feelings, and you'll learn how to do it.*

- If necessary, tell students where and when the next session will be.

Session 5 Claiming Your Feelings

Overview_____

The principal goal of this session is to help students understand what it means to own a feeling (claim it as their own). Students learn that once they own a feeling, they can begin to identify choices they have in dealing with it. "Talking things over with yourself" is introduced as a way to help identify feelings and understand options. Students also learn ways to step outside of feelings at times when their feelings are too powerful to deal with.

Learner Outcomes_____

The purpose of this session is to help group members:

- Understand that part of sticking up for themselves is claiming or "owning" their feelings.

- Understand that talking things over with themselves can help them learn more about their feelings.

- Identify ways to detach from or let go of feelings that are too strong to cope with at the moment.

Materials_____

- The student's book, *Stick Up For Yourself.* (Activities 2, 5)

- Chalkboard or flip chart. (Activity 3)

- Slips of paper with the name of one *low-intensity* or *high-intensity* feeling written on each (See page 17 of student text), and a sack to put them in. (Activity 3)

- Copies of the list found on page 101 in the Appendix for the role play. (See Activity 3)

- One copy for each student of the script for talking about feelings, found on page 102 in the Appendix. (Activity 4)

Agenda_____

1. Introduce the session.

2. Review the reading assignment.

3. Lead the role-play activity, "What Does It Mean to Claim a Feeling?"

4. Lead the activity, "Talking Things Over With Yourself," to help group members learn more about a feeling, on the spot, by having a conversation with themselves.

5. Lead the activity, "Great Escapes," to help group members identify their choices when they want to change the way they feel by detaching or letting go.

6. Close the session and assign reading.

Activities_____

1. Introduction

- Tell group members:

— *In this session, we'll continue talking about feelings. This session is about claiming your feelings. Naming and claiming your feelings helps you get to know yourself, another way to get personal power.*

2. Reading

- Ask the group to read pages 44 – 45 in *Stick Up For Yourself*.

- Ask:

— *What do the authors say about locking up feelings inside yourself or trying to push them away? Let's find that information and read it again.*

- Group members will find this information in the last two paragraphs on page 45 of *Stick Up For Yourself*. Ask someone to read the paragraphs aloud:

"You may try to push away some feelings, future dreams, and needs, or lock them up inside yourself. This isn't a good idea, because they don't stay away or locked up. They can turn into big problems later.

"Many adults today have big problems in their lives. Doctors think it's because they pushed away or locked up important feelings, future dreams, and needs when they were kids. When we do this, we lose track of who we really are. We lose our *selves*."

■ Say to the group members:

— *In this session, you'll learn ways to help you claim your feelings.*

3. What Does It Mean to Claim a Feeling?

■ Say to the group:

— *Let's take a couple of minutes to see if we can remember the names of feelings we talked about last session. Without looking in your book, can you think of one? Another one? Any more? Now look back at page 17 in your book. Which feelings did we miss?*

(Continue until you have the names of all 16 feelings on a chalkboard or flip chart.)

— *In the last session, we learned that it's important to know the names of feelings, because the names make it easier for us to talk about what we're feeling–whether we're talking to ourselves or to other people.*

■ Divide the class into small groups. Ideally, there will be no more than six people per group; eight would be okay.

■ Tell them:

— *We're going to play a game. I need one person from each group to come up and draw the name of a feeling out of this sack.*

— *Send somebody from your group to draw the feeling name. That person will become that feeling. For example, if you come up here and draw the feeling "Anger," you will be that feeling when you go back to your group.*

■ Hand out copies of a list of things that they might do when the person playing the role of the "feeling" returns to their group (a reproducible copy of the list is found on page 101 of the Appendix):

Claim it. (Your group decides who will claim the feeling.)
Ignore it.
Ask it to go away.
Tell it you'll think about it later.
Call it by some other name.

- Say:

  — *The rest of you have roles to play, too. One person in your group will claim the feeling. The rest of you will choose something else to do.*

  — *The person from each group who will draw the feeling name, come up here now. Draw your feeling and stay here for a few minutes.*

- Tell the groups:

  — *Each of you has to decide what you will do and say when the "feeling" comes and talks to you.*

  — *Only one person in your group can claim the feeling. Decide together, without giving it away, who will claim the feeling. That person must figure out a way to claim the feeling as a real part of him or her.*

  — *Choose from the list what you will do when the feeling comes up to you. More than one person can choose the same thing to do–except for claiming it.*

- Tell the "feelings" to return to their own groups. They are to go up to each person in the group, announce who they are, and make their faces look like the feeling. ("I'm angry," "I'm sad," and so on.)

- Tell the rest of the group members to be ready to act out their roles when the feeling comes up to them.

- After a few minutes, ask everyone to take their seats again.

- Ask the "feelings":

  — *What did people in your group say or do when they didn't want to claim you? What else? Anything else?* (List their responses on the chalkboard or flip chart.)

- Ask the group members:

  — *Who decided to ignore the feeling? Raise your hands. Was that hard to do? Why or why not?*

  — *If this really were* your *feeling, do you think it would go away that easily?*

  — *If you told a feeling to come back later, do you think it would come back at the right time?*

- Write on the chalkboard or flip chart:

If we claim a feeling, all it means is that we accept it. We own it as a part of us at that moment.

■ Conclude the activity by saying:

— *Claiming a feeling may be a lot easier than we think; we just need to take time to identify what we are feeling, to name it, and then to accept that we are feeling that way.*

— *Claiming a feeling doesn't mean we are stuck with it forever; it just means we know it's there and we own it.*

4. Talking Things Over With Yourself

■ Say to the group:

— *You can learn a lot about your feelings by talking things over with yourself. Today we're going to practice doing that.*

■ Give each group member a sheet with a script to use when talking things over with themselves. (You can make copies of the script found on page 102 in the Appendix.)

■ Say to the group:

— *Before you work on your own, let's look over the script on page 46 in our book to get some ideas of how to do this.*

— *Notice that your sheet has the same questions as the script in the book, but there are blanks so you can put in the name of your own feeling.*

— *Take a few minutes now and write about what you are feeling right at this moment. This is just for you; you won't have to share it with anyone else unless you want to.*

■ After a few minutes, ask the group:

— *What did you learn from doing this?*

— *Did anyone have trouble figuring out what you were feeling?*

— *Does anyone want to share what you found out about your feeling?*

— *Did anyone have trouble figuring out what to do about the feeling?*

— *Does anyone want to share what you decided to do about your feeling?*

— *Sometimes you can't change the feeling right away. It just takes time. But, by talking things over with yourself, you may get some ideas about what to do about the feeling or what causes it.*

- Conclude by saying:

— *Keep this script in your notebook to help you remember the questions to ask when you want to talk feelings over with yourself.*

5. Great Escapes

- Introduce the activity by saying:

— *We've all had feelings that were so strong we wanted to get rid of them. After we claim a feeling, we may decide we want to leave it for now because it seems too strong to deal with at the moment.*

- Tell the group:

— *In* Stick Up For Yourself, *the authors talk about four Great Escapes. Turn to page 48 so we can quickly review what the four Great Escapes are. Who can tell me what one of the four is? Another? A third? And the last? We're not going to talk about daydreaming in this course, but you may want to try it when you are at home.*

- Tell the group:

— *Someone here may already use one of these escapes.*

— *Does anyone use laughing as an escape? What do you find to laugh at?*

— *Does anyone use exercise–like swimming or biking or running–to turn your attention away from a feeling? How well does it work for you? In what type of situations do you use it?*

- Ask the group:

— *Sometimes we're in situations where we can't, right then, take a walk, or ride a bike, or find something to laugh about. It helps to have a way to escape a feeling, even when you can't escape the scene.*

— *Has anybody ever heard of Bubble Meditation?*

— *Is there anybody in this room who has blown bubbles using a wand and bubble soap? Then you know how much fun it is to blow a really large bubble and watch it float away .*

— *That's the idea of Bubble Meditation. Take a worry or feeling you need to be away from, put it inside a bubble, and let it float away for now.*

— *Let's try it for a few minutes to get an idea of how it works.*

- Say to the group:

— *Even if you don't have a feeling right now that you want to escape, you might have something that is worrying you. Each of us has something we worry about–even if it is just now and then. Let's use Bubble Meditation to help us get away from that worry.*

— *Sit comfortably in your chair, with your feet flat on the floor, and close your eyes.*

— *Take a few deep breaths. Breathe in through your nose, and breathe out through your mouth.*

— *Breathe in, breathe out. Breathe in, breathe out. Feel yourself relax.*

— *Think for a minute about something that has been bothering you lately–it might be anything, big or small.*

— *Picture yourself holding a huge bubble wand and a bottle of bubble soap. The bubble wand is as tall as you are, and the soap bottle takes up the whole corner of this room.*

— *Dip the wand into the bottle.*

— *Blow into the wand now. Watch a huge bubble start to form.*

— *As the bubble forms, imagine your worry going inside the bubble.* (Pause for 10–15 seconds.)

— *Watch the bubble float away, taking your worry with it.* (Pause)

— *Let it go.* (Pause)

— *Blow another bubble. Put another worry inside.* (Pause)

— *Watch it float away.* (Pause)

— *Let it go.* (Pause)

— *Blow another bubble. Put another worry inside.* (Pause)

— *Watch it float away.* (Pause)

— *Let it go.* (Pause)

- After several minutes, say:

— *Now take a deep breath, in through your nose, out through your mouth.*

— *Feel what it's like to have your worry gone for now. Open your eyes again.*

- Conclude by saying:

— *Different people have different ways of letting go of feelings. The next time you have a feeling that is too strong to deal with at the moment, think about one way you can get away from it until it seems more manageable. Later, come back to it, and talk it over with yourself.*

6. Session Closing

- Summarize by saying:

— *In this session, you learned that claiming your feelings is an important part of getting to know yourself.*

— *You learned that one way to claim your feelings is to talk things over with yourself.*

— *When feelings seem too strong to handle, you learned that you may need to step outside of the feeling and let it go for a while. We talked about some things you can do to help you let go of feelings.*

- Tell group members:

— *Before the next session, please read pages 32 – 36, 44 – 47, and 68 – 69 in* Stick Up For Yourself. *Next week, we'll be talking about what it means to name and claim your dreams.*

- If necessary, tell students where and when the next session will be.

Session 6

Naming and Claiming Your Dreams

Overview_____

This session is designed to help group members learn another way to get personal power–naming and claiming their dreams. The main concept presented in this session is that dreams are their personal goals. Dreams are important in developing personal power and positive self-esteem. Two kinds of dreams are discussed–near-future dreams and far-future dreams. Students learn how the two are related. They practice talking a dream over with themselves.

Learner Outcomes_____

The purpose of this session is to help group members:

- Understand that part of sticking up for yourself is naming and claiming dreams.

- Understand how talking things over with themselves can help them learn more about their dreams.

- Distinguish between near-future and far-future dreams.

- Identify the I-Did-It List as a way to build positive self-esteem.

Materials_____

- The student's book, *Stick Up For Yourself.* (Activities 2, 5)

- A chalkboard or flip chart. (Activities 2, 3)

- Students' notebooks. (Activities 3, 6)

- A volleyball. (Activity 4)

- A copy for each student of the script for talking dreams over with yourself (see page 103 in the Appendix for a reproducible copy). (Activity 5)

- A copy for each student of "Keeping Your I-Did-It List" (a reproducible copy is found on page 104 in the Appendix). (Activity 6)

Agenda

1. Introduce the session.

2. Review the reading assignment.

3. Lead the activity, "Naming Your Dreams."

4. Lead the game, "Dream Volley," to help group members practice relating near-future and far-future dreams.

5. Lead the activity, "Talking Things Over With Yourself," to help group members learn to make choices about their dreams by having a conversation with themselves.

6. Lead the activity, "The I-Did-It List."

7. Close the session and assign reading.

Activities

1. Introduction

- Tell group members:

— *In this session, we'll talk about naming and claiming your dreams, which is a way to get to know yourself. It is also a way to get personal power.*

2. Reading

- Ask the group to read pages 32 – 36 in *Stick Up For Yourself*.

- Tell them they'll read about a time machine exercise, but they won't be doing it right now. Recommend that they try it when they are at home.

- When they have had time to read, say to the class:

— *On page 34, the last paragraph includes something that is very important to know about future dreams. Who can tell me why future dreams are so important to us?*

- After someone has answered the question, read this part of the paragraph:

"Your future dreams are your personal goals. They give your life direction, purpose, and meaning. They guide your decisions and help you define the kind of person you are and want to be."

■ Say:

— *Let's reword the paragraph I just read, and find out how it affects us if we don't have future dreams.*

— *"If you have no future dreams you have no personal goals. You have nothing to give your life direction, purpose, and meaning. You have nothing to guide your decisions and help you define the kind of person you are and want to be."*

■ Write the following on the chalkboard or flip chart:

Having no dreams is like being a ship without a . . .

■ Ask:

— *Can you think of an ending for this sentence?*

(Examples: a ship without a sail, a ship without a rudder, a ship without a captain, or a ship without an ocean)

■ Conclude by saying:

— *In this session, you'll practice naming and claiming your dreams. Later you may want to take time to go back and do some of the activities you read about here today.*

3. Naming Your Dreams

■ Tell the group:

— *There are two kinds of dreams for you to think about–dreams for the near future and dreams for the far future. You need both kinds.*

— *Let's figure out first what we mean by near future and far future so that we're talking about the same thing. What do you think the near future is?*

(Discuss until you reach consensus.)

— *What do you think the far future means? When you have finished your education or job training? When you're thirty or forty?*

(Discuss until you reach consensus.)

— *I'd like to hear about some of your dreams for the far future. I'll tell you some of mine, too.*

   (Write a list of dreams on the chalkboard or flip chart as they volunteer.)

— *Now let's hear some of your dreams for the near future. I'll tell you some of mine, too.*

   (Write a list of dreams on the chalkboard or flip chart as they volunteer.)

— *Which list do you think has the "bigger dreams"–the far-future list or the near-future list? Does that make sense? Why or why not?*

— *Do you think our dreams for the far future and the near future need to be related? Why or why not?*

■ Say to the group:

— *In your notebook, as quickly as you can, write down 10 dreams you have. Don't think right now about whether they are for the far future or near future.*

— *You won't be asked to share these, unless you want to. They are just for you to know about.*

■ After allowing enough time for writing, say to the group:

— *Now, for each dream on your list, decide whether it is a near-future or far-future dream. Put an "N" beside those that are near-future dreams and an "F" beside those that are far-future dreams.*

— *Did you have both kinds of dreams on your list?*

— *Read to yourself one of your far-future dreams. Do you have a near-future dream to help make your far-future dream come true?*

— *Who has an example they'd be willing to share?*

■ Conclude by saying:

— *In this activity, we practiced naming our dreams. We learned that there are two kinds of dreams–far future and near future. We need both kinds.*

4. Dream Volley

- Clear an area of the room so you have enough space to have two teams positioned, as though they were on a volleyball court–a row by the net, a middle row, and a back row. The number of people you have in each column depends on the size of your group.

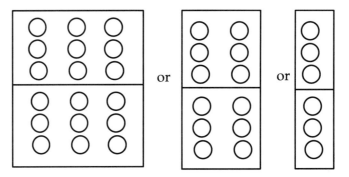

- Just as in a real volleyball game, students should rotate during play.

- Say to the group:

— *We're going to play a game called Dream Volley. It has some rules you have to learn, so listen carefully. Then you'll have a chance to ask questions.*

- Tell the group the rules:

— ***Rule No. 1.*** *In this game, just gently toss the ball to someone, instead of hitting it like you do in volleyball.*

— ***Rule No. 2.*** *Before you throw the ball, you will name a dream.*

— *If you're in the back row, your dream has to be a far-future dream. If you're in the middle row, your dream has to be a near-future dream. If you're in the front row by the net line, you can either name a near-future dream or a far-future dream.*

- Ask:

— *Do you understand so far? Near-future dreamers, raise your hands.* (The middle and front rows should raise their hands.) *Far-future dreamers, raise your hands.* (The back and front rows should raise their hands.)

— ***Rule No. 3.*** *The dream you name has to be related to the dream the person named who threw the ball to you. So if someone from the back row says, "I'm going to be a famous inventor," that is his or her far-future dream. Before you throw the ball to someone else, you have to name a dream that is related to the dream of being a famous inventor.*

— Who can think of an example of a near-future dream that would make sense for someone who wants to be an inventor?

(If they can't come up with any, mention that "doing well in science and math courses in high school" would be a near-future dream that is related.)

— Who can think of a far-future dream that would be related?

■ Ask:

— Do you understand the rules now? Any questions?

■ Say:

— Here's how we'll keep score. We'll have two judges at the net. If they put thumbs up, it means they think the answer related to the dream. The game can go on; nobody gets a point. If one or both of them put thumbs down, the other team gets a point. Understand? Okay, I need two judges; we'll be changing judges now and then, too.

(Appoint the judges.)

■ After a few minutes, stop the game, tell who won, and ask them to take their seats.

■ Say:

— You can see how hard it would be for us to always come up with dreams that match somebody else's dreams.

— There are people who spend most of their lives doing that very thing–trying to live out somebody else's dreams.

— It's important to begin understanding what your dreams are, and to make sure you have some near-future dreams that will help you reach your far-future dreams.

5. Talking Things Over With Yourself

■ Say to the group:

— You can learn a lot about your dreams by talking things over with yourself. Today we're going to practice.

■ Give each group member a sheet with a script to use when talking dreams over with yourself. (You can make copies of the script found on page 103 in the Appendix.)

- Say to the group:

— *Before you do this on your own, let's look over the script on page 47 in our book to get some ideas. The script for dreams is #2 at the top of the page.*

— *Notice that your sheet has the same questions, but there are blanks so you can put in the name of the dream you are talking over with yourself today.*

— *Take a few minutes now and write about a dream you have for the near future or far future. This is for you; you won't have to share it with anyone else unless you want to.*

- After a few minutes, ask the group:

— *What did you learn from doing this?*

— *Did anyone have trouble figuring out what you have to learn to make this dream happen? By talking things over with yourself, you may get some ideas about what you need to learn.*

— *Does anyone want to share their dream and tell us what they decided to do to help make their dream come true?*

- After allowing time for those who want to share, conclude by saying:

— *Keep a copy of this script in your notebook to help you remember the questions to ask when you want to talk things over with yourself.*

6. The I-Did-It List

- Say to the group:

— *Since the second session you have been keeping a Happiness List to help you collect good feelings.*

— *Today you're going to begin keeping an I-Did-It List. It is like the Happiness List, but instead of writing down things that happened, you write down things you did that that you feel proud of. Like activities you took part in. Problems you solved. Successes you had. Accomplishments of any kind. And anything else you feel satisfied with and good about.*

— *Right now, in your notebook write down five things you did yesterday that you feel good about.*

■ After they've had time to write, ask:

— *Did anybody get stuck trying to make a list? Maybe you were trying to find huge successes.*

— *Here are six things to do to help you get the most from your I-Did-It List.*

■ Hand out to each student a copy of "Keeping Your I-Did-It List" (a reproducible copy is on page 104 in the Appendix). Read it to the students, or ask them to read:

1. Notice the event when it occurs.
2. Feel the proud feeling.
3. Collect and store it inside you.
4. Write it down on your list.
5. Review your list at the end of the day.
6. Feel proud all over again.

■ Say:

— *Your list could include things like this:*

"I took out the garbage without being told."

"I fed the cat."

"I studied for my math test."

"I remembered to ask about make-up work."

■ Tell students:

— *Keeping an I-Did-It List helps you stick up for yourself–with yourself. It helps you gain personal power and build positive self-esteem from inside.*

— *Be proud of yourself at least 5 times every day.*

— *Being proud of yourself does not mean feeling that you are better than other people. It just means enjoying your own accomplishments, however small they are.*

— *Think of your I-Did-It List as a self-esteem savings account. It reminds you of how valuable and worthwhile you are.*

— *Do this every day, just like you do your Happiness List. Do it weekdays and weekends. School days and holidays.*

7. Session Closing

- Summarize by saying:

— *In this session you learned that naming and claiming your dreams is an important part of getting to know yourself.*

— *You learned that you need to have two kinds of dreams—near future and far future. Your near-future dreams can help your far-future dreams come true.*

— *You practiced talking things over with yourself as a way to figure out how to claim your dreams and begin identifying things to do that will help your dreams come true.*

— *You also learned about the I-Did-It List, a self-esteem savings account.*

- Tell group members:

— *Next session, we'll be talking about what it means to name and claim your needs. Before then, please read pages 36 – 47 in* Stick Up For Yourself.

- If necessary, tell students where and when the next session will be.

Session 7

Naming and Claiming Your Needs

Overview_____

This session is designed to help group members learn to name and claim their needs. Seven basic needs are presented: relationships with other people; touching and holding; belonging and feeling "one" with others; being different and separate from others; nurturing other people; feeling worthwhile, valued, and admired; and having power in our relationships and our lives.

Students learn that the more they know about their needs, the more they can understand them and tell other people about them. Knowing their needs and thinking of ways to get them met are important ways to stick up for themselves. They learn that their needs guide their decisions and help them define the kinds of people they are or want to become. They learn how their needs play a role when choosing and building relationships.

Learner Outcomes_____

The purpose of this session is to help group members:

■ Understand that part of sticking up for yourself is naming and claiming needs.

■ Identify seven needs that are common to all people.

■ Understand how talking things over with themselves can help them learn more about their needs.

Materials_____

■ The student's book, *Stick Up For Yourself.* (Activities 2, 5)

■ A copy for each student of the seven needs (see page 105 in the Appendix for a reproducible copy). (Activity 3)

■ A large, oblong piece of white paper to use to create a mural. (Activity 4)

■ Tape or glue to attach pictures to mural. (Activity 4)

- Magazines, catalogs, newspapers, drawing paper, and scissors. (Activity 4)

- A copy for each student of the script for talking about needs (see page 106 in the Appendix for a reproducible copy). (Activity 5)

Agenda

1. Introduce the session.

2. Review the reading assignment.

3. Lead the discussion, "What Do You Need?"

4. Lead the art activity, "Picture Your Need," to practice identifying how students' needs relate to what they do in their daily lives.

5. Lead the activity, "Talking Things Over With Yourself," to help group members learn to identify their needs at the moment, by having a conversation with themselves.

6. Review the reasons for keeping an I-Did-It List.

7. Close the session and assign reading.

Activities

1. Introduction

- Tell group members:

— *In this session, we'll talk about naming and claiming our needs, which is a way to get to know ourselves. It is also a way we get personal power.*

— *All human beings have the same basic needs. When our needs are met, we are healthier, happier people.*

— *Sometimes it's difficult to get certain needs met right now. In this session, we'll learn what we might be able to do, even when we can't get our needs met.*

2. Reading

- Ask the group to read or review the reading assignment, pages 36 – 47 in *Stick Up For Yourself.*

- When they have had time to read, ask:

— *What do we sometimes really mean when we say we* need *something, like "I* need *a haircut"?*

(They should respond that we really mean we *want* something.)

- Ask:

— *Is* needing other people *a sign we are strong or a sign we are weak? Find a sentence or two in your book that supports your answer and read it to us.*

(On page 37, the authors say: "If you need other people, if you have relationships with other people, then you aren't weak! *You're strong.* Needing is a source of strength.")

— *Why is it sometimes hard for people to get enough* touching and holding *in our society?*

(On page 38, students learned that in our culture touching and holding are often confused with sex.)

- Remind them that they need to be very clear about the difference between good touch and bad touch.

- Tell them that bad touch occurs when someone–usually a grownup or older child–touches you in a sexual way that feels bad or wrong, or in a way you don't want.

- Tell them to find an adult they trust and talk about good and bad touching if they are at all confused.

- Ask:

— *Why do you think we* need to feel we belong *and* need to become like other people?

(It helps us learn to be "human beings" when we model other people's behavior, starting when we are babies.)

— *At the same time that we need to belong, we also* need to be different and separate. *We go back and forth between these two needs.*

— *We* need to nurture *other people. It makes them feel good, and it makes us feel good inside.*

— *We all* need to feel worthwhile, valued, and admired. *If other people aren't helping us feel worthwhile, valued, and admired, who can do that for us?*

(You want them to say that this can come from other people, but it can also come from ourselves. We need to learn to encourage and affirm ourselves.)

— *We need to feel we have* power in our relationships and in our lives. *We'll talk about this need in the next session.*

■ Conclude by saying:

— *In this session, you'll practice naming and claiming your needs. Later, you may want to take time to go back and do some of the activities you read about here today.*

3. What Do You Need?

■ Before you begin leading this activity, hand out the "Seven Needs" sheet (a reproducible copy is on page 105 in the Appendix). Read it to the students, or ask them to read:

The need for relationships with other people

The need for touching and holding

The need to belong and feel "one" with others

The need to be different and separate from others

The need to nurture (to care for and help other people)

The need to feel worthwhile, valued, and admired

The need for power in our relationships and our lives

■ Tell the group:

— *If you need something, but you don't know what it is, how can you figure out what you need?*

(If someone suggests that you could try talking it over with yourself, agree with them, and say that we'll be practicing doing that later in the session.)

— *Do you think that our feelings or dreams might tell us something about our needs?*

- Say to the group:

— *What if I say to you, "I'm feeling lonely." What need might I have?* (Need to relate to other people; need for touching and holding; need for belonging)

— *If you dream of being in charge of your life, being able to make all your decisions without asking someone else for approval, what need might this be?* (Need for power in my relationships and in my life)

- Ask the group to come up with other feelings or dreams and relate them to needs. If they are having trouble, you might use one or more of the following to help the discussion:

  I don't like being in clubs and with my old friends right now. I want to spend more time on my own. What might I need? (I might be needing to be different and separate.)

  I'm having trouble seeing that anything I do really matters. What might I need? (I need to feel worthwhile, valued, and admired.)

  I wish I were little again for a day and could curl up in my dad's lap and listen to a story. What might I need? (I might need to be touched and held.)

- Conclude by saying:

— *In this activity, we practiced naming our needs. We learned that our feelings and dreams can help us learn something about our needs.*

4. Picture Your Need

- Put this title on the large piece of white paper you have available for a mural: "Picture Your Need."

- Have available a pile of old magazines, catalogs, and newspapers, some art paper for those who may want to draw a picture, scissors, and glue or tape.

- Say to the group:

— *We're going to make a mural.*

— *Each of you will find a picture in one of these magazines or newspapers. Or you can draw one yourself. There is drawing paper at the front of the room, too.*

— *Your picture should relate to one of the seven basic needs. It could be very obvious to us how it relates, or we may need to think a little before we identify the connection.*

— *We'll take 10 minutes to work on this.*

— *As soon as you find a picture, cut it out, and put it on the mural. Don't tell us about the need, though. Not yet. We'll try to guess first.*

■ After 10 minutes, tell the group to quickly put the magazines and other materials away.

■ Say to the group:

— *We're going to take a few minutes to see if we can guess the need that each of these pictures is about.*

   (**Note**: Take only about a half minute or so for each. Stop after five minutes.)

■ After guessing how an item relates to a need, ask the person who put the picture on the mural, "What need did you have in mind?"

■ Conclude by saying:

— *In this activity, you found pictures that reminded you of one of the basic needs. We're getting practice thinking about the basic needs and how they relate to our lives. If you didn't find a picture today, bring one to the next session and add it to the mural.*

5. Talking Things Over With Yourself

■ Say to the group:

— *You can learn a lot about your needs by talking things over with yourself. Today we're going to practice.*

■ Give each group member a copy of the sheet with the script to use when talking needs over with yourself. (A reproducible copy of the script is found on page 106 in the Appendix.)

■ Say to the group:

— *Before you do this on your own, let's look over a script in* Stick Up For Yourself *to get some ideas. The script for needs is #3, in the middle of page 47.*

— *Notice that your sheet has the same questions, but there are blanks so you can put in the name of the need you are talking over with yourself today.*

— *Take a few minutes and write about a need you have right now. This is just for you; you won't have to share it with anyone else unless you want to.*

■ After a few minutes, ask the group:

— *What did you learn from doing this?*

— *Did anyone have trouble figuring out what to do to help yourself get this need met? By talking things over with yourself, you may get some ideas.*

— *Does anyone want to share their need and tell us one thing they decided to do to help get the need met?*

■ After allowing time for those who want to share, conclude by saying:

— *Keep a copy of this script in your notebook to help you remember the questions to ask when you want to talk needs over with yourself.*

6. The I-Did-It List (Review)

■ Say to the group:

— *In the last session, you learned about the I-Did-It List, and I asked you to start keeping the list every day, just like you do the Happiness List.*

— *How is it going? Are you finding things you feel satisfied with and good about to put on your list? Are you able to be proud of yourself five times every day?*

— *Did anybody get stuck trying to make a list? Were you trying to find huge successes? It's important to focus on* anything *you did that you are proud of, or any difficult situation you handled well enough.*

■ Say:

— *It may take a while for you to easily notice your successes. We sometimes train ourselves to notice the things we don't do well. That gets in the way of noticing our successes.*

— *Just keep writing each day, and soon it will get to be a habit.*

— *Remember, this is like a self-esteem savings account. Don't let it be empty. It reminds you how valuable and worthwhile you are. And that's one of the seven basic needs!*

7. Session Closing

■ Summarize by saying:

— *In this session, you learned that naming and claiming your needs is an important part of getting to know yourself.*

— *You learned that there are seven basic needs that everybody has.*

— *You practiced talking needs over with yourself as a way to figure out how to get a need met.*

— *You also heard a reminder about how important it is to keep writing your I-Did-It List.*

■ Tell group members:

— *Next session, we'll be talking about what it means to get and use power in your relationships and in your life. We'll learn the difference between personal power and role power.*

— *Before the next session, read pages 51 – 60 in* Stick Up For Yourself.

— *(**Optional**) Also, for an activity we'll do next week, if you know of a song that you think says something about personal power, please bring a tape or record with the song for us to listen to.*

■ If necessary, tell students where and when the next session will be.

Session 8 Getting and Using Power

Overview

This session is designed to help students learn the difference between role power and personal power. Role power is something they have because of what they do (their role). Personal power is something they have because of who they are. Personal power is the most important kind of power they'll ever have. It means they can have power over their own lives, even if they never have much role power.

Through discussion activities, students learn to identify choices they have in situations in which they may have thought they were powerless. Identifying choices is presented as a way they can help themselves feel they have power in their lives.

Learner Outcomes

The purpose of this session is to help class members:

■ Understand the differences between role power and personal power.

■ Understand that their feelings help them recognize whether people are using power in a positive or negative way.

■ Understand that their feelings help them recognize whether they are using power over other people in a positive or negative way.

■ Understand that when they are given choices, they feel powerful instead of powerless.

■ Identify choices they can give themselves that will help them feel they have power in their lives.

Materials

■ The student's book, *Stick Up For Yourself.* (Activity 2)

■ Chalkboard or flip chart. (Activities 2, 3)

■ Students' notebooks. (Activity 3)

■ *(Optional)* A record player and a tape player. (Activity 4)

Agenda

1. Introduce the session.

2. Review the reading assignment.

3. Lead the discussion, "Two Kinds of Power," to identify differences between role power and personal power.

4. *(Optional)* Lead the activity, "Power Tune," to let them hear songs that talk about power.

5. Lead the activity, "Balance of Power," to identify ways to develop equal power in a relationship.

6. Review the Happiness List and the I-Did-It List.

7. Close the session and assign reading.

Activities

1. Introduction

- Tell the class:

— *You may remember that personal power has four parts. We've already talked about three of those parts–being responsible for your feelings and behavior, making choices, and getting to know yourself. In this session, we're going to talk about the fourth part–getting and using power in your relationships and your life.*

— *This session will help you identify ways you already have power in your life, as well as new ways to use your personal power.*

2. Reading

- Ask the class to read or review the reading assignment, pages 51 – 60 in *Stick Up For Yourself*.

- When they have had time to read, ask:

— *What are the two kinds of power the book talks about?* (Personal power and role power)

- Ask the following questions, and write the students' answers on a chalkboard or flip chart:

— *Who can tell me one difference between role power and personal power?*

— *What's another difference?*

— *Are there any more differences?*

— *Any more?*

- Give students time to mention the four differences discussed in the book on pages 52 and 53. They are shown below:

"Role power is something you get 'just because.' Personal power is something you get because you *want it* and you *work for it*.

"Role power depends on having someone else to be powerful over. (A king without people to rule doesn't have much role power.) Personal power depends on you and only you.

"Role power is something you might have to wait for. You might never have very much role power. Personal power is something you can have *right now*, if you want it. And you can have as much as you want.

"Only some people can have role power. Anyone can have personal power. You can have personal power. *Even if many people have role power over you.*"

- Ask:

— *Why is it a big waste of energy to always fight back against people who have role power over you?* (It probably doesn't do any good; it might even be getting you in trouble. You have to accept that there will *always* be people with role power over you.)

— *What can you do with your energy instead of fighting back?*

- Conclude by saying:

— *In this reading, you learned there are two kinds of power. Personal power is by far the most important kind of power you'll ever have. It means you can have power over your life, even if you never have much role power.*

3. Two Kinds of Power

■ Tell students:

— *Think of role power as power you have not because of who you are, but just because of what you do–in other words, your role.*

— *Right now, there are people in our lives who have role power over us. This is true for all of us.*

■ Tell them briefly about people that have role power over you–and why they have role power.

■ Ask students to take out their notebooks and divide a page into two parts by drawing a line (show them how on the chalkboard or flip chart):

Role power over me	How I feel about it

■ Tell them to title the columns "Role power over me" and "How I feel about it."

■ Tell them to list the people who have role power over them right now in their daily lives. They can write the person's name, or the person's role–like parents, math teacher, and so on.

■ Ask them to write a word or two in the second column that describes how they feel about that person's role power over them. Suggest some words that they might use: Okay, So-So, Crummy, No Problem, Super. (Or, they could use ++, +, –, or – –.)

■ Give them a few minutes to work on their lists.

■ Ask:

— *Do you feel the same way about all the people who have role power over you?*

— *Why do you think it feels okay when some people use role power over you, and not okay when others do?* (You want them to discover that it depends partly on what it is they ask you to do, and how they treat you.)

- Ask:

— *Choose one person on your list.*

— *If you could switch roles and have role power over the person who you chose, what would you do the same as that person? Why? What would you do differently? Why?*

— *Who would like to share your thoughts?*

— *If you can decide how you wish the person with role power would change, it might help you identify what you need to work on accepting.*

- Conclude by saying:

— *The way we treat people when we have role power has a lot to do with whether or not we have personal power. That's another reason that getting to know yourself and getting personal power will be important to you always.*

4. Power Tune (optional)

- Have available a tape player and a record player. You will select one or more songs (as time allows) to play. It is a good idea to preview them so that you can be sure the lyrics are compatible with your program's standards (e.g., avoid sexist, racist, and violent lyrics).

- Tell students:

— *Last week, I mentioned that if you had a song that you thought was about personal power, you could bring it for us to listen to. I'm going to play a couple of those songs now. As you listen, see if you can identify what the song has to do with personal power.*

- After listening to each song, ask:

— *What words in the song do you remember?*

— *What message do you think this song has about personal power?*

- Conclude by saying:

— *There are many ways our culture talks about power. Songs are one way. Art is another way. Advertising is another way. Begin noticing power images. When you see or hear one, think about whether it is about personal power or role power.*

5. Balance of Power

— (**Note**: This activity could be expanded. Instead of having each group talk about equal power in only one context — i.e., with a friend, sibling, or peer group — you may want to schedule another session or sessions so that each group can talk about situations in all contexts. This would give students a greater opportunity to incorporate the ideas of developing equal power in all their relationships.

Surprising or threatening feelings might be raised when you are talking about power in relationships, even feelings about how students perceive their teachers using role power over them. Be aware of your own feelings, and take time later to be sure you have paid enough attention to what you were experiencing.)

■ Ask:

— *If you were going to give a friend power over you, how would you do it?* (Possible answers: always do what they want to do, always say what they want to hear.)

■ Say:

— *Sometimes we give friends power over us, and we don't even know we're doing it. Our feelings can help us become aware of times we are giving away our power, or when we have power over other people.*

— *We're going to divide into 5 small groups. In your group, you will be talking about a time when you felt that you did not have equal power with someone else; it may even be an example of a time when you felt totally powerless.*

■ After dividing them into small groups, say:

— *Group 1, you will be talking about situations that are with a* friend.

— *Group 2, situations with your* peer group.

— *Group 3, situations with a* sibling.

(Be sure members of this group all have siblings; if not, exchange members with another group until everyone in this group has a sibling.)

— *Group 4, situations with a* teacher.

— *Group 5, situations with a* parent.

- Say:

— *I want someone in each group to volunteer to start by giving one example of a situation in which you don't feel you have equal power or in which you feel powerless. Say how you feel when you're powerless (ashamed, angry, etc.). Then, ask your group for suggestions about how you could develop equal power with this person or group. Identify as many realistic choices as you can.*

— *Be sure to keep it moving so that everyone in your group has a chance to participate.*

- After a few minutes, bring them back together, and ask:

— *I need one volunteer from each group to describe a situation that was discussed and tell what the group suggested.*

- When the volunteer has finished telling about the situation, ask:

— *How many of you have been in this kind of situation?*

— *Does anyone have any other suggestions to make? If not, we'll go on now.*

- Continue until you have heard at least one person from each group.

- Conclude by saying:

— *In this activity, we talked about ways to help us overcome the feeling that we are powerless, and to develop equal power. It's important to learn to focus on what we have power over and choices we can make, instead of trying to change other people.*

6. The Happiness List and I-Did-It List (Review)

- Say to the group:

— *How are you doing with your Happiness List and I-Did-It List?* (Share with them some of the things you've been noticing since you began keeping your own lists.)

— *Are you finding things to put on your list that you feel satisfied with and good about–things that made you smile? Is it getting to be a habit to notice things that make you happy?*

— *Is it getting easier to identify five things you did each day that you feel proud of?*

- Remind them of the six steps for each list:

— *Notice the event when it occurs.*

— *Feel the good (or proud) feeling.*

— *Collect and store it inside you.*

— *Write it down on your list.*

— *Review your list at the end of the day.*

— *Feel good (or proud) all over again.*

- Say:

— *The important thing is to just keep writing your lists each day, and soon it will get to be a habit.*

— *The Happiness List is your collection of good and happy feelings. Don't stop collecting.*

— *Your I-Did-It List reminds you how valuable and worthwhile you are; when your self-esteem is strong, you will feel your personal power.*

7. Session Closing

- Summarize by saying:

— *In this session, you learned there are two kinds of power: personal power and role power.*

— *You talked with each other about ways to develop equal power in a relationship.*

- Tell group members:

— *In the next session, we'll be talking about learning to like yourself.*

— *Before then, read pages 65 – 76 in* Stick Up For Yourself.

- If necessary, tell students where and when the next session will be.

Session 9 Learning to Like Yourself

Overview_____

This session focuses on developing positive self-esteem. Students begin to understand and identify how their inner voices influence their self-esteem. They learn that sometimes their inner voices, i.e., what they are thinking or feeling or imagining about themselves, have a great impact on their self-esteem. They learn that they can become aware of those inner voices and learn to change them, so that the judgments they are continuously giving themselves about themselves are positive and self-affirming.

Students also think about things they can begin doing every day to be good to themselves and take care of themselves.

Learner Outcomes_____

The purpose of this session is to help class members:

- Understand that they need positive self-esteem in order to stick up for themselves.

- Identify good things about themselves.

- Understand how to change critical, blaming, and comparing inner voices into self-affirming inner voices.

- Identify good things to begin doing for themselves.

Materials_____

- The student's book, *Stick Up For Yourself*. (Activities 2, 3)

- Students' notebooks. (Activities 2, 3)

- Two pieces of paper for each student; a sack. (Activities 4, 6)

- Chalkboard or flip chart. (Activity 4)

- A copy for each student of the handout titled "Six Things to Do for Yourself." (A reproducible copy is found on page 107 in the Appendix.) (Activity 5)

Agenda

1. Introduce the session.

2. Review the reading assignment.

3. Introduce the self-esteem quiz on pages 66 – 67 in *Stick Up For Yourself*, and have students take it.

4. Lead the role-play activity, "Time to Talk Back," to help students learn to change negative, critical inner voices into self-affirming inner voices.

5. Lead the activity, "Six Things to Do for Yourself," to give students an opportunity to identify ways they can be good to themselves and take care of themselves.

6. Ask students to write role-play scenarios for next week's final session.

7. Close the session.

Activities

1. Introduction

■ Tell group members:

— *In this session, we'll focus on positive self-esteem. In order to stick up for yourself, you need to feel good about yourself, to feel valuable and worthwhile.*

— *We'll practice some tools that will help you develop positive self-esteem.*

2. Reading

■ Ask someone in the group to read aloud the introductory part of page 65 in *Stick Up For Yourself*.

■ When they are finished, ask them to take out their notebooks and quickly write five good things about themselves that they would tell the alien.

■ After they have had time to write, tell them:

— *All of today's reading has to do with ways to improve your self-esteem. We'll be practicing some of the activities the authors suggest to help build positive self-esteem.*

3. Listening to Your Inner Voices

- Tell students:

— *We're going to take a few minutes to do the self-esteem self-quiz on pages 66 and 67. I'll read the questions out loud. Then you choose the letter of the answer that is closest to the way you talk to yourself, think about yourself, or feel inside yourself. Write the answer letter, a or b, in your notebook.*

— *If you would rather read to yourself, go ahead. If you just want to listen and then write the answer, a or b, you can do that.*

- After students take the quiz, tell them how to score it:

— *Count all of your "a" answers, and multiply the number of "a" answers by 10.*

— *Now count all of your "b" answers, and multiply by 5.*

— *Add the two scores together. Look at the key on page 68 to find out what your score suggests about your self-esteem.*

- Say:

— *You don't need to share your score with anyone. It is for your own information.*

- Ask:

— *How many of you agree with how your self-esteem is rated using this quiz?*

- Say:

— *Remember, you're in charge of your life, and that includes your self-esteem. If your score is low, don't worry about it. You're already working on it. You're practicing one important way to help strengthen your self-esteem—the I-Did-It List.*

- Tell students:

— *Before we leave the self-esteem quiz, we're going to look at some of the possible answers in the quiz one more time.*

— *Turn to the quiz on pages 66 and 67 of your book.*

— *Sometimes we blame or criticize ourselves. If we do this a lot, it lowers our self-esteem. Some of the answers in the quiz are examples of how we might be blaming or criticizing ourselves.*

— *Let's find an example of the kind of thing we would say to ourselves if we were blaming ourselves. Read the answers until you find one that you think is an example of blaming. What did you find?*

— *Now find one that you think is criticizing. What is it?*

— *Can you find another blaming or criticizing answer?*

(If they are having trouble, you may want to suggest they read the "b" answers.)

— *Think for a minute about yourself–do you blame or criticize yourself? A little bit? A lot? Now and then? You don't need to tell us your answer. Just think about it.*

— *In addition to blaming and criticizing ourselves, another thing we sometimes do is compare ourselves with other people. When we compare, we often end up feeling that somehow we don't measure up–other people are smarter, or better looking, or they run faster, or they have more friends.*

— *If we spend a lot of time comparing, we may end up thinking we are not a valuable, worthwhile person unless we are better than someone else in some way.*

— *Can you find an answer in the self-esteem quiz that shows someone comparing himself or herself with another person?*

(If they have trouble identifying one, ask them, "How about number 5?")

— *Do you ever compare yourself with other people? Do you do it a lot? Again, just think about it; you don't have to answer out loud.*

■ Conclude by telling the students:

— *In the self-esteem quiz, there were examples of things people sometimes tell themselves about themselves.*

— *Blaming, criticizing, and comparing are the three shaming voices we found examples of. We learn to treat ourselves in these ways. We're not just born doing it. But we can change this behavior.*

— *In the next activity, we're going to find out how we can feel better about ourselves by talking back when we hear ourselves blaming ourselves, criticizing ourselves, or comparing ourselves with other people.*

4. Time to Talk Back

- Tell students:

— *What do you think an inner voice is?*

(You want them to say that it is the way we talk to ourselves–including the things we tell ourselves *about* ourselves. It's how we treat ourselves, how we behave toward ourselves in ways that produce positive or negative feelings.)

- Tell students:

— *You can change your inner voice from a negative to a positive voice by doing several things. Let's write them on the board to help us remember them:*

By having new words to say to yourself

By having new feelings of love and respect for yourself

By imagining an inner voice that is like the voice of someone you respect and admire

- Ask:

— *Can you think of one thing you sometimes tell yourself about yourself that is blaming or criticizing?*

— *I'm going to hand out a slip of paper to each of you; I want you to write on your paper one thing you say to yourself when you're being hard on yourself. When you're done, come up here and put your slip of paper in this sack.*

- When they are done, take a minute to silently read through them.

- Say:

— *Boy, we have a lot of negative things that we tell ourselves. One of the things I catch myself saying to myself is, "You're so _____.*

(Fill in the blank with what you say to yourself–impatient, stubborn, forgetful, clumsy.)

- Say:

— *I'm going to write 5 things you mentioned on the board.*

- Say:

— *We can train ourselves to change those negative inner voices that say things to us like these five things. Let's practice.*

- Say:

— *First, let's think about* new words. *To begin to change your inner voices, if you have been saying something like this to yourself, what new words might you say to yourself instead?*

— *Next, let's think about* new feelings *to help us have positive inner voices. What have you been doing in this course that might help you remember happy or proud feelings and memories?*

(Keeping a Happiness List and an I-Did-It List.)

— *These feelings and memories can help you change your inner voices.*

— *Finally, let's try to* imagine new inner voices *that are like the voices of people who like us and encourage us. Do you have someone in mind who you might imagine saying something helpful to you, something encouraging? Imagine what this person might say to you when you are thinking this thought; now tell yourself those words. Actually imagine this other person speaking inside of you. Visualize this person saying the new words and expressing the new feelings toward you.*

— *Who can think of someone whose voice would be a nice model for your inner voice? Does anyone want to tell us who they are thinking about?*

- Conclude by saying:

— *The next time you are aware of a negative inner voice, try to remember the things that can help you change to a positive inner voice.*

— *New words to tell yourself, new feelings, and comforting, encouraging affirming voices inside you will help you build positive self-esteem.*

5. Six Things to Do for Yourself

- Hand out the sheet of paper that has the six things described on pages 73 and 74 of *Stick Up For Yourself*. (You can make copies of the reproducible sheet which is found on page 107 in the Appendix.)

- Say:

— *This is your homework assignment.*

— *Think of something for each of the six items; fill it in and bring it to the next session. We'll be talking about it then.*

6. Writing a Role-Play Scenario

- Hand out a piece of paper to each student.

- Tell students:

— *In this course, we've been learning new ways to stick up for ourselves. Next week, in our last session, you're going to role-play ways to stick up for yourselves, using your own role-play ideas.*

— *I want you to write about something that is happening in your life in which you would like to learn to stick up for yourself. You don't need to put your name on the paper.*

- If they're having trouble thinking of something, give them a couple of examples.

- After giving them time to write, collect their papers. Conclude by saying:

— *Next week, we'll role-play as many of these as we have time for, to give you new ideas about how to stick up for yourselves.*

7. Session Closing

- Summarize by saying:

— *In this session, you learned some ways to strengthen your self-esteem.*

— *You took a quiz to determine how your self-esteem is right now, and you thought about whether you agree or disagree with the score. Either way, you know that you have the I-Did-It List as a tool to help you build positive self-esteem.*

— *Each of you thought of one way that you criticize yourself. You took turns thinking of how to change a negative voice into a positive, self-affirming voice. Positive inner voices are important to your self-esteem.*

- Tell students:

— *Next session is the last one for this course.*

— *Before the next session, do your homework assignment and continue writing your Happiness List and I-Did-It List.*

- If necessary, tell students where and when the next session will be.

Session 10

Sticking Up for Yourself from Now On

Overview_____

This final session reviews the ways students have been learning in this course to stick up for themselves. Through role play, students are able to demonstrate their understanding of the various tools they can use to stick up for themselves.

Learner Outcomes_____

The purpose of this session is to help class members:

- Review the tools they learned to use in this course: the Happiness List, the I-Did-It List, and Talking Things Over With Yourself.

- Demonstrate, through role-playing, ways to stick up for themselves.

- Evaluate their progress toward their goals, which they described in writing in Session 1, Activity 6.

- Evaluate the course as a whole.

Materials_____

- A copy of the scripts on pages 102, 103, and 106 in the Appendix, for you to refer to in "Keep Talking Things Over With Yourself." (Activity 4)

- Students' notebooks. (Activities 4, 7)

- Students' homework assignments from Session 9, Activity 5. (Activity 2)

- One role-play idea for each pair of students, written on a piece of paper (use scenarios your students developed during Session 9, Activity 6, and/or use the role-playing scenarios which are found on page 108 in the Appendix); a box or sack. (Activity 6)

■ A copy of a course evaluation form for each student; you need to decide in advance what to use for the evaluation. You may want to read "Evaluation Suggestions" on page 3. There is a sample course evaluation form on page 109 in the Appendix. (Activity 8)

Agenda_____

1. Introduce the session.

2. Review the homework assignment from Session 9, Activity 5, "Six Things to Do for Yourself."

3. Lead the discussion, "Our Lists–Another Look."

4. Lead the activity, "Keep Talking Things Over With Yourself."

5. Lead the activity, "One New Thing I Do to Stick Up for Myself."

6. Lead the role-play activity in which students help each other identify ways to stick up for themselves.

7. Ask students to do a self-evaluation of their progress in the course. They will read the goals that they wrote during the first session and decide whether or not they met their goals.

8. Ask students to evaluate the course as a whole.

9. Close the session.

Activities_____

1. Introduction

■ Tell group members:

— *In this final session, we'll review some of the things we've learned in the course.*

— *We'll also be doing some role-playing to help each other find new ways to stick up for ourselves.*

2. Six Things to Do for Yourself

■ Say:

— *In the last session, you had a homework assignment. Let's find out how that went.*

— *Take out the assignment sheets on which you listed six things you could do for yourself this week.*

■ Ask:

— *Who would like to tell us what you did just for fun this week?*

— *Which of you gave yourself presents? Would you like to tell us what you gave yourself? Was it hard to think of a present to give yourself every day? How might you make it simpler?*

— *Did you forgive yourself for something you did in the past? Why do you think it's important to forgive yourself?*

— *What did you do that was good for your body? Did anybody decide to eat differently? Get more sleep? Do you know how much sleep is recommended for people your age?*

— *How did you take care of your brain? Did you find something new to read, or think about, or look at, or listen to each day?*

— *Maybe you found an adult to talk to, someone who could help you answer some questions, or who was willing to listen to something that was on your mind. Does anyone have anything to say about that?*

■ Conclude by saying:

— *Remember, one way to stick up for yourself is to take care of yourself. The way we take care of ourselves one day may be different than what we need to do to take care of ourselves the next day. The important thing is to keep at it. It is something that will be important throughout your entire life.*

3. Our Lists—Another Look

■ Tell the class:

— *We can teach ourselves to notice things we do and to be proud of them. What is one thing we learned to do in this course that helps us notice and take credit for what we do each day?*

(You want them to mention the I-Did-It List.)

— *Why is it important to collect good feelings? How can we do that?*

(You want them to talk about the Happiness List.)

— *Don't forget, your lists are important. Continue to add to them.*

— What if you have a feeling you want to collect, or you do something you're proud of, but you don't have a notebook with you at the time? (Think about it; write it down as soon as you have a chance.)

— Even if you don't carry a notebook around, you could stick a piece of paper in your pocket to use for your lists.

■ Encourage them to find notebooks that they can carry and use during the day. You may want to show them some small notebooks–maybe some that you have used to keep your lists. Or show them sheets of paper you've written on. Tell them there are many kinds of small notebooks they can easily carry in a pocket or in a purse or school bag.

■ Tell the class:

— Plan your time so that you can review your lists during the last few minutes before you go to bed at night, and feel the happy and proud feelings all over again.

4. Keep Talking Things Over With Yourself

(**Note**: You may want to refer to the scripts found on pages 102, 103, and 106 in the Appendix as you lead this activity.)

■ Tell the class:

— What can we talk over with ourselves? (Feelings, needs, dreams)

— Can anybody tell me how we go about talking things over with ourselves? Let's start with feelings. How might we go about talking over a feeling with ourselves? How would we start? What question could we ask? (How am I feeling today?)

— After you name the feeling, what can you ask? Find the script in your notebooks, if you need help remembering. (When you know the feeling, you ask, "Why am I feeling ____? What's happened that I feel ____ about? Then ask what you can do about the feeling.)

■ Follow the same procedure and review the process for talking over needs and dreams with yourself.

■ Conclude by reminding the students that even though they can't always find someone else to talk to at the moment they need to, they can do a lot for themselves by talking things over with themselves.

5. "One New Thing I Do to Stick up for Myself"

- Ask:

— *I'm going to go around the room, and I'd like each of you to tell me one new thing you are doing to stick up for yourself with others.*

— *Now I'm going to go around the room and ask you to tell me one new thing you are doing to stick up for yourself with yourself.*

(If someone can't think of anything to say, you might ask, "Are you doing anything differently when you make mistakes?")

- Encourage them to practice noticing ways they are sticking up for themselves, and then to tell themselves they're doing a good job.

- Tell them they can learn by watching how other people stick up for themselves. Tell them that the role play you'll do next may give them some more ideas about how to stick up for themselves.

6. Role-Playing

- Tell students:

— *Last week, you each wrote about a situation in which you would like to learn to stick up for yourself. Today we're going to role-play some of those situations, to help us learn from each other.*

- Divide the class into pairs. Each pair will do at least one role play. They may do more, depending on the size of your group and the amount of time you have available.

- Ask someone from each pair to come up and draw a piece of paper. (Have each role-play idea on a separate piece of paper in a box or sack.)

- Tell them:

— *Read about the situation you will role-play, then decide who plays which role. You will have a few minutes to rehearse.*

- After a few minutes, bring the class back together. Ask for volunteers to go first. Tell them to read the scenario out loud, then do the role play.

- After each role play, ask the class:

— *Do you understand what they are suggesting you could do to stick up for yourself in this situation? What is clear? What isn't clear?*

- After discussing, thank the role players, then go on to another role play. Continue the same procedure, role-playing and discussing, until all the pairs have participated.

- Ask:

— *Did you learn at least one new way to stick up for yourself? Do you have an idea where you might try it out?*

- Conclude by saying:

— *We are all role models for each other.*

— *We can learn a lot from each other. We still have to make our own decisions because we are responsible for our feelings and behavior. But it helps to get ideas from other people.*

7. Student Self-Evaluation

- Tell the students:

— *During the first session, you set a goal for yourself for this course and you described it in writing in your notebook. Now I want you to find that page in your notebook.*

— *You wrote an ending to this sentence: "In this course, I want to learn new ways to stick up for myself when . . ."*

— *Take a few minutes and write, on the same page, any new ways you've learned to stick up for yourself. This is just for you; you don't need to share it with anyone else.*

- Ask students:

— *How many of you think you met your goal?*

- Remind them that change takes time. It's okay to recognize that they're not where they want to be yet, without feeling that they've failed themselves.

8. Student Course Evaluation

- Give each student a copy of a course evaluation form.

- Tell students:

— *I want to find out some things about how you felt about this course as a whole. I'm going to give you each a form. Please tell me what you want me to know about the course. It will help me when I teach the course to another group of students. If you need more room to write, you can use the back of the sheet.*

9. Session Closing

- Summarize by saying:

— *In this course, you learned new ways to strengthen your self-esteem and stick up for yourself. You have some tools you can use every day, and we reviewed those in this session—the Happiness List, the I-Did-It List, and Talking Things Over With Yourself.*

- Tell the students:

— *Thank you for your part—sharing your feelings and thoughts, and helping each other learn new ways to stick up for yourselves. Remember, change takes time. Keep practicing the tools you've learned.*

— *You can keep on developing personal power and positive self-esteem by sticking up for yourself with yourself and with others.*

ADDITIONAL
ACTIVITIES

ADDITIONAL ACTIVITIES

Curriculum-Related Activities . . . .

The activities in this section allow you to reinforce concepts students are learning in this course.   They are related to curriculum areas.

*Language Arts
and Creative Writing*

1. In a novel or short story, ask students to find examples of ways the writer lets us know what the characters are feeling.

    Give these examples:

    He looked down at the ground as he walked. His hands were in his pockets.
    What might he be feeling?

    She was practically skipping down the hall.
    What might she be feeling?

    John looked at his test results, and said, "Oh, yes!"
    What might John be feeling?

2. Ask students to write a paragraph that describes a feeling, without using the feeling name.

Social Studies

1. Ask students to find pictures of people in newspapers and magazines. Ask them to identify what they think the people in the pictures might have been feeling when the picture was taken.

2. Mention to students that good politicians know that one way to get public support is to get people's feelings involved in an issue. Ask them to watch the evening news and try to find an example in which a politician may have been trying to "trigger" a certain feeling. Ask them to tell the group what the politician said that made them think it was an attempt to get people to feel a certain way about the issue.

3. Find headlines in newspapers or magazines that use names of feelings or convey feelings.

4. Have students do research to find out if people in various cultures express their feelings in the same ways.

Art	To help students learn how to draw nonverbal clues that show behavior, ask them how they would draw inanimate objects so they look like they have feelings. Divide them into groups, and ask them to come up with ideas. Here are some ideas: an angry pencil, a sad house, a depressed table, a furious lamp.
Music	Ask students to bring a tape which has a song that always makes them feel happy. Use the songs they bring as background music during another group activity.
Other Languages	Have students translate the names of feelings into another language that they are studying or would like to study. Tell them to make a poster showing the word in English and in as many other languages as they can find.

Social Activities . . . .

An important part of this course is the social interaction among the students. During the course, you may want to have social activities that extend beyond the regular session time, and this section gives you some ideas.

Breaks	During breaks, you may want to encourage students to get to know someone they don't already know. Tell the students you will have a "Spotlight Minute" after the break. This can be a signal that anyone in the group can tell something interesting they learned about someone else during the break.
Parties	Plan a party for the end of the course. Ask volunteers to help plan it. Ask the volunteers to make up a recipe for the party which tells each class member what to bring to the party. Here's an example: 1 joke, 1 board game, a small can of pop, 2 snacks to share.
Phone Calls	When students are making new friends, they sometimes find it scary to make phone calls to each other. You may want to have an assignment in which each student exchanges phone numbers with one other person. During the week, they are asked to call up the other person and say, "Hello!" and "How's it going?" Tell them to decide who will call first.

Ask them to think about what they might talk about.

Ask them why they sometimes feel nervous about making a phone call. (For example, they might think the other person won't be glad to hear from them; or they might be afraid someone else will answer the phone.)

APPENDIX

Dear Parents,

I am writing to tell you about a course that we will begin soon. It is a ten-session course to help students develop positive self-esteem. I am excited about the course, and I want to tell you about it.

The course teaches students how to be responsible for their feelings and behavior. Through readings and activities, they learn what it means to stick up for themselves and how to go about it by making choices, by getting to know and like themselves, and by developing their relationships with other people. A list of the topics we will cover is enclosed.

You may want to read the text your children will be reading. I encourage you to do that. Students who have already taken the course think that is a good idea. It will help you know what we will be discussing. The text is titled *Stick Up For Yourself! Every Kid's Guide to Personal Power and Positive Self-Esteem*, by Gershen Kaufman, Ph.D. and Lev Raphael, Ph.D. I will mention to the students that you may be borrowing the text to read, and I will encourage them to take it home with them. (If you want to look at the text before the course begins, please let me know and I'll arrange that.)

Students want their parents to *know about* the course, but they may not always want to *talk about* it while they are taking it. It's a good idea to let them bring it up. Feel free to call me with any questions you have, before the course begins–or during the course. My phone number is on the bottom of this letter.

This can be a wonderful growing experience for your young person. You may notice that your young person is "trying on" new behaviors, new ways of relating to you or others in the family–maybe talking about things that are important. Sometimes new behaviors are awkward; change takes time. You may see a new behavior one day and then wonder where it went the next day. When this happens, it might help to think about those times in our adult lives when we try to make changes. Changing is often very slow for us, too.

Students have different levels of comfort when talking about feelings. They can choose to participate in the discussions, or to pass if they don't want to share their feelings. Either is okay.

Please call me if I can clarify anything about the course.

Sincerely,

P.S. You can reach me at _____ . Convenient times to reach me are

_____ . The class begins on _____ .

Stick Up For Yourself

Session Topics and Reading Assignments

Session	Reading
1 What Does it Mean to Stick Up for Yourself?	ix – xi
2 You Are Responsible for Your Behavior and Feelings	1 – 7; 61 – 63
3 Making Choices	8 – 13
4 Naming Your Feelings	14 – 31
5 Claiming Your Feelings	44 – 50
6 Naming and Claiming Your Dreams	32 – 36; 44 – 47; 68 – 69
7 Naming and Claiming Your Needs	36 – 47
8 Getting and Using Power	51 – 60
9 Learning to Like Yourself	65 – 76
10 Sticking Up for Yourself from Now On	

Questions for Role Play

Where is your homework?

Why didn't you call like you said you would?

Why did you wear my sweater without asking?

Who told you that you could do that?

What happened to the change?

Why are you late?

Why aren't the dishes washed?

Who broke this?

Tell me why your grades dropped.

Keeping Your Happiness List

- Notice the event when it occurs.

- Feel the good feeling.

- Collect and store it inside you.

- Write it down on your list.

- Review your list at the end of the day.

- Feel the good feelings all over again.

Session 5 (Activity 3)

Things To Do

- Claim it. (Your group decides who will claim the feeling.)

- Ignore it.

- Ask it to go away.

- Tell it you'll think about it later.

- Call it by some other name.

Talking Things Over With Yourself

(Talking About Feelings)

Ask yourself, "How am I feeling today?" Then name a feeling you're having.
Next, talk it over with yourself. Your talk might go like this:

SAY: **ASK:**

I'm feeling _____
today.

                                                 Why am I feeling _____?
                                                 What's happened that I
                                                 feel _____ about?

I'm feeling _____
because:

_____

_____

                                                 What can I do about my

                                                 _____ feeling?

                                                 _____

                                                 _____

I can _____

_____

_____

Talking Things Over With Yourself

(Talking About Dreams)

Ask yourself, "What are my future dreams?" Then name a dream for the near future or the far future. Next, talk it over with yourself. Your talk might go like this:

SAY: **ASK:**

I really want to

_____

someday.   What do I have to learn to make
                                                          this dream happen?

I can start by:

_____

_____

_____   What will I actually do?

I can:

_____

_____

_____

Keeping Your I-Did-It List

- Notice the event when it occurs.

- Feel the proud feeling.

- Collect and store it inside you.

- Write it down on your list.

- Review your list at the end of the day.

- Feel proud all over again.

Seven Needs

The need for relationships with other people

The need for touching and holding

The need to belong and feel "one" with others

The need to be different and separate from others

The need to nurture (to care for and help other people)

The need to feel worthwhile, valued, and admired

The need for power in our relationships and our lives

Talking Things Over With Yourself

(Talking About Needs)

Ask yourself, "Is there anything I need right now?" If yes, try to name your need. Then talk it over with yourself. Your talk might go like this:

SAY: **ASK:**

I need to:

_____

                                                    How can I start to get that need met?

I can start by:

_____

_____

_____

                                                    What if that doesn't work?

I can:

_____

_____

_____

Six Things to Do for Yourself

1. Choose something to do *just for fun.* Then do it whenever you can.

2. Give yourself a "present" every day.

3. Forgive yourself for something you did in the past.

4. Do at least one thing every day that's good for your body.

5. Do at least one thing every day that's good for your brain.

6. Find an adult you can trust and talk to.

My Plan for This Week:

One thing I might do just for fun is

_____

One present I might give myself is

_____

One thing I might forgive myself for doing is

_____

I can do this for my body

_____

I can do this for my brain

_____

I will think of an adult I can trust and talk to when I need to talk things over. One person I'm thinking of is

_____

Scenarios for Role-Playing

These scenarios were written by students taking the course, Stick Up For Yourself.

- You are at a movie, and the person behind you is loud and annoying.

- A teacher doesn't give you the full directions, and you don't get a good grade because of it.

- Your parents try to blame you for something you didn't do.

- Your parents break a promise.

- A friend says that your entry in a contest was dumb.

- Someone in your class always bugs you and calls you names.

- Someone teases you about the boy (girl) you like.

- You are with a group of friends. They are planning to get even with someone who did something they didn't like. You tell your friends you want to stay out of it, and they get mad at you.

- The teacher asks a question. You raise your hand, and nobody else does. The teacher won't call on you.

- Your coach doesn't give your team any credit for trying.

Stick Up For Yourself

Student's Course Evaluation

1. Circle the answer that tells how often you are keeping a Happiness List.

   Every day   Most days   Now and then   Never

2. Circle the answer that tells how often you are keeping an I-Did-It List.

   Every day   Most days   Now and then   Never

3. What is one way you have learned to stick up for yourself?

   _____

   _____

4. I am talking things over with myself about my feelings.

   Every day   Most days   Now and then   Never

5. I am talking things over with myself about my dreams.

   Every day   Most days   Now and then   Never

6. I am talking things over with myself about my needs.

   Every day   Most days   Now and then   Never

7. I am more aware of my inner voices.

   Every day   Most days   Now and then   Never

8. The tool that was most helpful in this course was

   _____

9. The thing I learned the most about in this course was

   _____

10. I wish there had been more _____ in this course.

11. I wish there had been less _____ in this course.

12. Do you have any other comments or suggestions? Write them on the back of this sheet.

Stick Up For Yourself
Parent's Course Evaluation

1. Have you observed any changes in your child's behavior since he or she has been taking this course? In particular, is there anything you have noticed that makes you think your child is developing new ways to stick up for herself or himself?

    If you feel comfortable in doing so, please describe what you have observed.

    _____

    _____

2. Did your child bring home the book, *Stick Up For Yourself,* and give you a chance to read it?

    Yes   No

3. Did you read the student's book, *Stick Up For Yourself?*

    Yes   No

4. Did your child talk to you about what we were discussing in the course?

    Every day   Most days   Now and then   Never

5. Did your child tell you about the Happiness List and I-Did-It Lists that we were keeping?

    Yes   No

6. Do you feel that this course was a good experience for your child? Why or why not?

    _____

    _____

7. What do you think is important for us to tell parents about the course?

    _____

    _____

8. Do you have any other comments? Write them on the back of this page.

RESOURCES

RESOURCES

Alberti, Robert E. and Emmons, Michael L. *Your Perfect Right: A Guide to Assertive Living.* San Luis Obispo, CA: Impact Publishers Inc., 1982.

Chase, Larry. *The Other Side of the Report Card: A How-to-Do-It Program for Affective Education.* Glenview, IL: Scott, Foresman & Co., 1975.

Clarke, Jean I. *Self-Esteem: A Family Affair.* New York: Harper & Row Publishers, Inc., 1980.

Kaufman, Gershen. *Shame: The Power of Caring.* Cambridge, MA: Schenkman Books, Inc., 1980.

Kaufman, Gershen, with Raphael, Lev. *The Dynamics of Power: Building a Competent Self.* Cambridge, MA: Schenkman Books, Inc., 1983.

Koch, Kenneth. *Wishes, Lies and Dreams: Teaching Children to Write Poetry.* New York: Harper & Row Publishers, Inc., 1980.

Stock, Gregory. *The Kids' Book of Questions.* New York: Workman Publishing Co., Inc., 1988.

Wells, Harold C. and Canfield, Jack. *One Hundred Ways to Enhance Self Concepts in the Classroom: Handbook for Teachers and Parents.* Englewood Cliffs, NJ: Prentice Hall, 1976.

How Are You Feeling Today? Poster. Cincinnati, OH: Creative Therapy Associates, 1989.

NOTES

NOTES

MEET THE AUTHORS

Gerri Johnson received her B.A. degree from Kansas Wesleyan and M.S.Ed. from the University of Kansas. She is sole proprietor of Mark My Word, a St. Paul, Minnesota, company specializing in instructional design and writing. Earlier in her career, she taught in elementary and junior high schools in California, Kansas, and Minnesota and at the University of Kansas and Pacific Lutheran University. She has published articles in regional and national publications and has served as project editor and ghost writer for numerous educational publications.

Gershen Kaufman was educated at Columbia University and received his Ph.D. in clinical psychology from the University of Rochester. Currently he is a professor in the Counseling Center at Michigan State University. He is also the author of *Shame: The Power of Caring* (Cambridge, Massachusetts: Schenkman Books, Inc., 1985) and *The Psychology of Shame: Theory and Treatment of Shame-Based Syndromes* (New York: Springer Publishing Co., 1989). He is the coauthor with Lev Raphael of *Dynamics of Power: Building a Competent Self* (Cambridge, Massachusetts: Schenkman Books, Inc., 1983).

Lev Raphael was educated at Fordham University and received his MFA in Creative Writing from the University of Massachusetts at Amherst. He holds a Ph.D. in American Studies from Michigan State University, where he has taught as an assistant professor of American Thought and Language. A prize-winning writer, he has published over two dozen short stories in magazines including *Redbook*, *Commentary*, and *Midstream*. With Gershen Kaufman, he co-developed and co-taught the program, "Psychological Health and Self-Esteem," on which *Dynamics of Power: Building a Competent Self* and *Stick Up for Yourself!* are based.

MORE FREE SPIRIT BOOKS

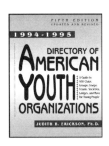

1994-1995 Directory of American Youth Organizations: *A Guide to 500 Clubs, Groups, Troops, Teams, Societies, Lodges, and More for Young People*
by Judith B. Erickson

A comprehensive, annotated guide to national, adult-sponsored, nonprofit youth organizations in the United States. Lists dozens of different types of groups, including special interest, sports, religious, conservation, political, ethnic heritage, and academic to name a few. Ages 6 and up.

$18.95; 200 pp.; s/c; 7 1/4" x 9 1/4"

Doing the Days: *A Year's Worth of Creative Journaling, Drawing, Listening, Reading, Thinking, Arts & Crafts Activities for Children Ages 8–12*
by Lorraine Dahlstrom

A total of 1,464 fun learning activities linked to the calendar year. Spans all areas of the curriculum and stresses whole language, cooperative learning, and critical thinking skills. Grades 3–6.

$21.95; 240 pp.; illus.; s/c; 8 1/2" x 11"

Fighting Invisible Tigers: *A Stress Management Guide for Teens*
by Earl Hipp

Advice for young people who feel frustrated, overwhelmed, or depressed about life and want to do something about it. Ages 11 and up.

$9.95; 120 pp.; illus.; s/c; 6" x 9"

Also available:

A Teacher's Guide to Fighting Invisible Tigers: *A 12-Part Course in Lifeskills Development*
by Connie Schmitz with Earl Hipp
$16.95; 144 pp.; s/c; 8 1/2" x 11"

Kidstories: *Biographies of 20 Young People You'd Like to Know*
by Jim Delisle

Inspiring biographies about real kids today who are doing something special to improve their lives, their schools, their communities, or the world. Includes questions to think about and resources for readers who want to know more. Ages 10 and up.

$9.95; 176 pp.; B&W photos; s/c; 6" x 9"

Making the Most of Today
Daily Readings for Young People on Self-Awareness, Creativity, and Self-Esteem
by Pamela Espeland and Rosemary Wallner

Quotes from figures including Eeyore, Mariah Carey, and Dr. Martin Luther King, Jr. guide young people through a year of positive thinking, problem-solving, and practical lifeskills. Ages 11 and up.

$8.95; 392 pp.; s/c; 4" x 7"

Psychology for Kids: *40 Fun Tests That Help You Learn About Yourself*
by Jonni Kincher

Based on sound psychological concepts, this fascinating book promotes self-discovery, self-awareness, and self-esteem. Helps young people answer questions like, "Are you an introvert or an extrovert?" and "What body language do you speak?" and empowers them to make good choices about their lives. Ages 10 and up.

$11.95; 160 pp.; illus.; s/c; 11" x 8 1/2"

Stick Up for Yourself! *Every Kid's Guide to Personal Power and Positive Self-Esteem*
by Gershen Kaufman, Ph.D. and Lev Raphael, Ph.D.

Realistic, encouraging how-to advice for kids on being assertive, building relationships, becoming responsible, growing a "feelings vocabulary," making good choices, solving problems, setting goals, and more. Ages 8–12.

$8.95; 96 pp.; illus.; s/c; 6" x 9"

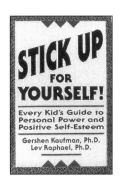

Understanding LD (Learning Differences): *A Curriculum to Promote LD Awareness, Self-Esteem, and Coping Skills in Students Ages 8–13*
by Susan McMurchie

Based on Free Spirit's *Survival Guide for Kids with LD* and *School Survival Guide for Kids with LD*, this comprehensive curriculum of 23 lessons helps students with LD become more aware of their learning differences and more positive about their capabilities. Includes dozens of reproducible handouts.

$21.95; 160 pp.; s/c; 8 1/2" x 11"

To place an order, or to request a free catalog of SELF-HELP FOR KIDS® materials, write or call:

Free Spirit Publishing Inc.
400 First Avenue North, Suite 616
Minneapolis, MN 55401-1730
toll-free (800)735-7323, local (612)338-2068